In this time, we find ourselves in an epic war over the nation of America—a spiritual war that greatly affects what occurs in the natural. Mike Thompson, in *The Lion's Army*, gives profound and revelatory insight into how this spiritual war is waged against believers and how the army of the Lion of Judah must, from a position of victory, be equipped to effectively dismantle and nullify the weapons of the kingdom of darkness and to neutralize those deploying them. Mike Thompson has been gifted to see in the realm of the Spirit in a way that shines a spotlight on this historic spiritual war. Be sober minded and vigilant, for the enemy roams about as a lion, seeking whom he may devour.

—Amanda Grace
Prophet; Bible Teacher
Founder, Ark of Grace Ministries

We all are drawn to the supernatural realm because as born-again believers we are part of it. *The Lion's Army* plays a crucial role in God's kingdom, carrying out a great commission. However, we cannot truly participate in that unless we learn to operate in the realm of the Spirit. The good news is that Mike Thompson has a remarkable way of explaining how we can become part of this powerful Lion's army. It's not a mystery—Mike shows you how you can become one of God's lions.

—Kathie Walters
Prophet; Author; Speaker
Founder, Kathie Walters Ministry

The Lion's Army is so apropos for today. What the Lord showed Mike through visions and visitations is being played out in our lives right now. I suggest that you buy two copies—one to give away and the other to keep so you can go back to reread and study. Better yet, it would be great to gather a group of people and study this book together.

This book will give you great confidence for the coming years. It can be shocking to realize that the scriptures you've studied for so long are being fulfilled in real life right now. We need to be vigilant and ready for end-time events. The best part is that Mike not only assures us of divine protection but also shows us the great power we possess to resist and destroy the wiles, or strategies, of the devil! Learning to walk and live in the Spirit is not just necessary in these last days—it is imperative.

There is too much richness of truth to summarize the contents of this book in just a few lines. You will not regret reading what Mike has laid out for our safety and growth!

—Dan Thompson, PhD
Pastor, Faith Builders Family Church

The book *The Lion's Army* deals with the subject of spiritual authority. The first traces of this subject in church history can be found in John A. MacMillan's book *The Authority of the Believer*. Decades later, Kenneth E. Hagin received further revelation on the subject and wrote his book *The Authority of the Believer*. He expanded on it in an updated version, titled *The Believer's Authority*.

In 1963 Kenneth E. Hagin experienced an open vision. In that vision, he saw a dark cloud covering the United States, representing communist atheism overtaking the nation. Hagin asked God if there was a remedy. The Lord showed him a ball of fire that broke apart and landed on an army of believers. Those believers then went throughout the earth, taking that fire to the masses.

In Mike Thompson's latest book, he further describes this army of believers, which he calls the Lion's army. The book details the army's characteristics and function, which Thompson received through divine revelation over the years. Mike's previous book, *Third-Heaven Authority*, along with his latest, *The Lion's Army*, continues this much-needed teaching on how the church needs to take its God-given authority in today's troubled world.

—JOSEPH MARTIN
AUTHOR; REVIVAL HISTORIAN

THE
LION'S
ARMY

MIKE THOMPSON

 CHARISMA HOUSE

While the author has made every effort to provide accurate, up-to-date source information at the time of publication, statistics and other data are constantly updated. Neither the publisher nor the author assumes any responsibility for errors or for changes that occur after publication. Further, the publisher and author do not have any control over and do not assume any responsibility for third-party websites or their content.

For more resources like this, visit MyCharismaShop.com and the author's website at mikethompsonministries.org.

Cataloging-in-Publication Data is on file with the Library of Congress.
International Standard Book Number: 978-1-63641-430-0
E-book ISBN: 978-1-63641-431-7

1 2024
Printed in the United States of America

Most Charisma Media products are available at special quantity discounts for bulk purchase for sales promotions, premiums, fund-raising, and educational needs. For details, call us at (407) 333-0600 or visit our website at charismamedia.com.

I dedicate this book to CK, my loving wife, best friend, and constant source of inspiration. Our journey together in the ways of the Spirit brings me strength and joy.

I give special thanks to my son Bryan for helping me carve out the time I needed to complete this project, and to Max Davis for the spiritual insight and expertise in bringing this manuscript to life.

CONTENTS

FOREWORD

By Eric Metaxas

ONE OF THE main reasons I'm so grateful for the ministry of Mike Thompson is that he is fulfilling God's calling on him to raise up the remnants of God's people into the mature believers God wants them to be. This book is a big part of that. Of course what Pastor Thompson is doing in what he teaches—in this book and in his previous book, *Third-Heaven Authority*, and from the pulpit too—is simply what we call discipleship. It is an inexpressibly vital part of Christian faith. Without it we will always be spiritual children, which is certainly not God's plan for His church.

But nothing has become clearer to me than the facts that discipleship has fallen on hard times and that most Christians are indeed not living anything close to the mature Christian lives the Lord intends for us to live. As

Mike Thompson makes clear, we are called to be prayer warriors! We are called by God to know our authority in Jesus and to walk in that authority so we can do what God longs for us to do—as well as be part of helping God's will manifest here on earth as it is in heaven! Can we imagine that God would call us to that? It's an astonishing privilege.

But most Christian leaders and pastors themselves are unaware of the deeper things of God. Many are even openly hostile to these things. This tragic misunderstanding has manifested itself in innumerable ways, but at the heart of it all is the obsession with a shallow evangelism at the cost of real discipleship. So we have millions of Christians in America who may be saved—we sincerely hope that they are—but who are not living out their faith in every sphere of life, who are still drinking milk and not eating meat, as Paul said in 1 Corinthians 3:1–3.

As I have written about in my recent book *Letter to the American Church* and the sequel, *Religionless Christianity*, these baby Christians have the false and decidedly unbiblical idea that the only thing that matters is salvation, which amounts to agreeing to a few theological ideas and then perhaps leading others to salvation. But there is infinitely more to the Christian life that God wants us to know about and experience. Mike Thompson delves into those deeper things. He has decades of practical experience in those things, as you will see from the stories he tells, but he also has the tremendous gift of being able to communicate from those experiences so that the rest of us can benefit. That's an especially rare gift.

So for that gift—and for Mike Thompson's indefatigable faithfulness in teaching on these deeper things—my gratitude to the Lord is genuinely boundless. With Mike

Thompson's help, God is raising up a mature, end-time remnant for His purposes in history, and we get to be a part of that. *Hallelujah!*

My favorite parts of this book are the amazing stories that Mike tells, all which are of course true and faith building. It's deeply encouraging to read about what God has done, and I'm particularly grateful that Mike has included these stories. But I'm also grateful for the earlier parts of this book, in which Mike is in solid teaching mode. Some of those earlier parts may be a little tougher to get through than the stories, which is why I highly recommend reading this book as a devotional so that you can set aside ten or so minutes each morning to read what it says, to reflect on it, and to pray.

Get ready to step into the next part of the adventure that the Lord has for you. It is a tremendous privilege that we get to be part of what God is doing in history for His eternal purposes. Buckle your seat belts, brethren.

And *rejoice*!

—ERIC METAXAS
NEW YORK TIMES BEST-SELLING AUTHOR; SPEAKER;
HOST, THE NATIONALLY SYNDICATED
ERIC METAXAS RADIO SHOW

Chapter 1

THE LION'S ARMY

I T WAS THE night of October 3, 2018, and a group of believers had assembled for our Samuel School of Supernatural Ministry. The subject of the module was "Third-Heaven Authority," and a thick anointing was already hanging heavily in the room. As I made my way to the podium, a familiar sense enveloped me—the sense that something supernatural was about to occur. I knew the indicators. The Holy Spirit had released the first of them earlier, as I prepared for the class.

Now, as I stood staring at the attendees, the spiritual realm began swirling around me, drawing me in. I could feel its tug as faint spiritual sounds and images caught my attention. Just before a spiritual encounter I typically experience these kinds of signs bleeding through the veil, from the spiritual realm into the physical realm. However, I was still not completely sure what would become of it, so I remained open to the Spirit, careful not to move impulsively.

After gathering myself and welcoming the class, I shared

from the podium an outline of the dynamic, enlightening things we were about to cover. Not more than ten minutes into the lesson, the spiritual swirling around me strengthened. Images of darkness were shattered by lightning forming in front of me. I could hear what sounded like muffled voices engaging in some sort of conflict. Glimpses of swords momentarily appeared. Something was up, and I knew the Lord was about to reveal an important truth.

As this experience unfolded, I told the class I was being pulled into a vision, and I asked them to pray. As they lifted their voices to the Lord, the vision fully opened before me. Suddenly, I found myself in a lofty place looking down on a large battlefield. Positioned over one end of it, I saw the field stretch out in front of me. On the far end a horde of hideous and grotesque demons with angry faces scowled and hissed, anxiously awaiting the call to attack. Then the ravenous mob released barrages of bloodcurdling screams and shrieks as it charged toward my end of the field. Although I was not personally afraid, their violent rage caused my body to shudder.

Simultaneously, the illumination came to me that the demons' shrieks and screams were their weapons. Their power was in menacing, frightening, intimidating, bullying, and abusing. Though the warfare was mostly psychological, it was clear that the mob would use physical violence if necessary. Their goal was to disrupt normalcy, to knock people off balance, and to cause them to question themselves and their beliefs.

Behind the screams, I detected and even smelled a hidden fear in the atmosphere around the demons. Putrid odors and unpleasant feelings can sometimes manifest when confronting the demonic, whether during a personal encounter or a vision. In this case the demons' fear was so strong that it caused them pain. They were afraid of losing and having to suffer the consequences brought by their own leader, as well as by their vanquishers. So they screamed louder, attempting to cover their dread.

Captivated by the scene playing out before me, I wondered, "What could all this mean?" No sooner had the question formed in my thoughts than a voice different from my own said, "These are the shriekers and screamers."

Just then the sound of a ferocious roar shook me to my core. It came from behind me, to my right. When I turned toward it, I was amazed to see a massive Lion, both majestic and terrifying. Yet my spirit knew that His wrath was not directed toward me. This Lion was *for* me, not against me. No doubt He was Jesus, the Lion of the tribe of Judah mentioned in the Book of Revelation when "one of the elders said to [John], 'Do not weep. Behold, the Lion of the tribe of Judah, the Root of David, has prevailed to open the scroll and to loose its seven seals'" (Rev. 5:5).

Gathered in front of the Lion was an immense army of righteous warriors clad in full armor with their swords held high, the light of God reflecting off them. This was the Lion's army of born-again, Spirit-filled believers. Strangely, as they stood before the Lion, not only did His roar thunder, but there were words in the roar, and both the roar and the words entered the backs of those in the righteous army. As I watched from aboe while all this unfolded, I had the distinct awareness that I was also one of the warriors below.

When the words penetrated the warriors' backs, the words came out of their mouths even as the Lion declared, "You have lost. We have won!" The Lion spoke this unanimous decree of victory through His army of righteous warriors. He possessed the ability to see the future outcome and then to infuse His warriors with that knowledge. A spiritual bond allowed them to work harmoniously with Him; the Spirit of God from the Lion was in His warriors.

Then the Spirit of God lifted the righteous army up and over the heads of the advancing horde of shriekers and screamers. I was amazed at the strategy! It demonstrated what the Lord showed me in 2010 when He took me to heaven and told me to teach third-heaven authority to His people. It was warfare from heaven's perspective, looking down from above rather than looking upward from the earth.

Then my view shifted to that of a warrior in the righteous army, which the Spirit had lifted above the shriekers and screamers. Looking down on the demonic horde, with one voice we warriors all shouted, "You have lost. We have won!"

We also spoke faith-filled proclamations and decrees and launched God's Word against the demons' screams. While proclaiming those words, we, the Lion's army, were binding, loosing, decreeing, and issuing forth our authority. Not only that, but the words came out of our mouths as flames of fire, with warring angels inside the flames! As this was happening, the Word of God came to me: "Who makes His angels spirits and His ministers a flame of fire" (Heb. 1:7). The angels appeared to not only carry fire but also respond to the fire that the warriors released. The angels guided the flames to the demonic targets without missing or hitting the ground.

Just as the Lion's army had angels and the fire of authority in their words, the shriekers and screamers had evil power in their screams. To combat this, the Lion's warriors used the righteous power He had given them as fire in their mouths—fire ignited by His truth. The spoken Word of God was a weapon, and the Lion delegated it, along with the authority to use it, to His army.

At this point in the vision a series of brief thoughts floated through my mind:

- If God's power is in the fire, it will lead to people getting saved and experiencing every possible kind of miracle.

- What the enemy does on the battlefield is meant to affect people on the earth. These demonic influences are what Paul called "this present evil age" (Gal. 1:4).

- What we are accomplishing here in the spirit realm will bring deliverance to the masses.

As I pondered these thoughts, angels and rapid-fire flames battered the demon forces, weakening and paralyzing them one by one. Then, without warning, a furious giant beast arose behind the advancing horde of demons and stood tall, much as the Lion of the tribe of Judah stood tall behind His righteous army. Knowing there was power in the demonic screams, the giant beast shouted out his orders: "Scream louder! Yell harder!"

But it was too late. The steady pounding from the Lion's army was taking its toll. The shriekers and screamers knew they were being defeated. As their demeanor slumped, an awareness came over me—I sensed that more demons stood in the shadows, awaiting the beast's call to engage.

Sure enough, I looked and saw two more hordes waiting on the left and right sides of the beast.

As the vision faded, I could feel myself coming back into the physical realm. Yet I remained in that place of spiritual consciousness for a few more minutes. Then the Lord spoke again, saying, "This is happening in the spiritual atmosphere over America. Do not be afraid, for the Lion's army is well equipped for the battle."

Although the vision receded, I felt instinctively that the revelation would be progressive and that more would unfold when the Lord was ready.

"Light Be!"

On January 8, 2021, while I engaged in prayer, the unfolding of more began. I wasn't asking for or seeking an encounter, yet the Lord once again opened the spiritual realm for me. Before I share any more, however, I feel it's necessary to clearly and briefly explain what happens to me when I'm pulled into this kind of full vision.

These encounters do not occur as mere pictures in my mind's eye or as some form of heightened imagination. I see the images as an HD movie, sometimes as though I'm there in person. These open visions are real to me and most often occur while I am already in prayer. But there are times when they begin as I am preaching or engaged in some other activity. The first indicators are an anointing that comes upon me and a heaviness I can feel on my body as my inner man is pulled into the spirit realm. The Holy Spirit enables my spirit to superimpose my spiritual senses and faculties over my physical ones. At this point I may briefly see sights or hear sounds that catch my attention.

As I yield to the Spirit and focus on these details, the vision unfolds before me.

To illustrate this process, I've often used the analogy of the heads-up display in my car, which is similar to what fighter pilots have used for years. The analogy is not perfect, but I believe it is helpful. My car's display reflects various bits of information onto the windshield. They include the posted speed limit, my current speed, my direction, the stereo settings, and certain navigational information. While driving, I'm looking through the information that is displayed, but my focus is on the road. Similarly, when I'm in an open vision, I can faintly see what's happening in the physical realm, but I'm focused on the vision.

With my spiritual thoughts and emotions fully engaged, the Holy Spirit paints the vision on my spiritual sight, hearing, smell, taste, and touch. Whether my eyes are open or shut, I watch the whole thing play out like a movie. This is biblical. In Acts 10:10, for example, we see that while Peter was praying on a housetop, "he fell into a trance." Then again, in Acts 11:5, while praying in Joppa, "in a trance [he] saw a vision." In both cases the Greek word translated "trance" is *ekstasis.* It denotes "'a state of mind when the attention is absorbed in a particular train of thought, so that the external senses are partially or entirely suspended.'...The soul seems to have passed out of the body, and to be conversant only with spiritual essences."[1] This describes what I experience.

You can't make a vision such as this happen. Sometimes I just watch the vision; at other times I'm an active participant. Either way, I am allowed some form of communication with the Holy Spirit or angels. While the vision is happening, I almost always sense an urging to pray or bind and loose. When the vision ends, there's usually a lag, as I'm simultaneously caught in both the heavenly and physical realms. The anointing eventually lifts, and the shift back to my outer man becomes complete. But later on, my memory of the encounter can pull me back into the anointing that accompanied the original vision.

All this is important because the Lion's army visions came to me in four separate installments before the Lord was done. Several times in my life I have experienced progressive visions in which the Holy Spirit added new installments. This was one of those times. As I was praying on January 8, 2021, the entire first vision played out before me just as it had before, but this time it continued from where the last one ended. The giant beast turned to his left and said to the fresh demons waiting in the wings, "The shriekers and the screamers have done their job, but they're faltering. You go forward."

So the fresh demon troops went in among the shriekers and the screamers. The demons' appearances were different from the first horde's appearance. They weren't hideous or scary but humanlike. Except for their sinister smiles, the demons' faces seemed almost normal. And as they moved into position, the beast told them, "Deceive. Bewitch."

The demons readily obeyed, and behind their malevolent smirks I could sense an almost tangible contempt for those who would be deceived. The air around the demons was disgusting, yet I knew that what seemed obvious to me could be confusing and deceptive to some people. The beast's orders were meant not only to deceive but also to spiritually bewitch. When I heard the command "Bewitch," Paul's words to the church in Galatia came to mind: "O foolish Galatians! Who has bewitched you that you should not obey the truth?" (Gal. 3:1). In this verse

Paul referenced how evil spirits can cause a fascination or spell-like deception that blinds people to the truth.

Fully aware of all that was happening, the Lion firmly countered the beast and his hordes, saying, "Lying unity—the army of lying unity, false unity, ungodly unity, and unity of the flesh!"

The Lion was speaking of the unity that tries to deceive people into naively aligning with whatever agenda the enemy puts forth. It's a deceiving unity. The word *unity* was being used as a kind of trance word to bewitch people into thinking that accepting the enemy's agenda would bring peace. But that was a lie. Unity of the Spirit as described in Ephesians 4:3 brings the peace of God, not just calmness in circumstances.

Perhaps the most devilish part of the beast's strategy was his knowledge that many in the Lion's army would fall for the deception. Why? Because they believed that God would allow whatever seemed to remove strife and bring calm, regardless of the source. I was aware that this was also true about people in society. The war being fought was designed to control the general public, and deception was a key weapon.

In the vision, amid the deception, the Lion announced, "Those who have experience in warring with lying unity, come forward."

With that the righteous army began adjusting its formation. The mature and experienced warriors moved to the front line, while the less experienced fighters shifted to the rear positions. Those now in the vanguard had experience with lying unity and had discerned how to effectively war against it. By their example, the others would follow and learn to spot the deception.

Positioned with those in the very front, I remembered something the Lord told me when I was a young minister: "One of the most overlooked spiritual gifts is discerning of spirits. Without it the other spiritual gifts can build a wonderful ministry that could be blown up by someone with a hidden, deceptive agenda. Develop discerning of spirits in your ministry!"

Paul mentioned the discerning of spirits in his first letter to the church at Corinth.

> For to one is given the word of wisdom through the Spirit, to another the word of knowledge through the same Spirit, to another faith by the same Spirit, to another gifts of healings by the same Spirit, to another the working of miracles, to another prophecy, to another *discerning of spirits*, to another different kinds of tongues, to another the interpretation of tongues.
>
> —1 CORINTHIANS 12:8–10

When the Lion of the tribe of Judah spoke again in the vision on January 8, 2021, His thunderous words came through the righteous warriors: "You have lost. We have won! Fellowship with darkness is prohibited."

The righteous army responded to these words by saying, "Light be!"

At that moment, the fire that had come out of their mouths against the shriekers and screamers changed into a brilliant light. Revelation, illumination, and truth came forth, and there were warring angels in the light, just as there had been angels in the fire. As the light came down onto the heads of those participating in lying unity, they began to weaken. Truth had the power to break their deception.

INFUSED WITH THE GLORY OF GOD

Twenty days later, on January 28, 2021, the Spirit of God pulled me into yet another open vision of the Lion's army. Just as before, I witnessed the righteous warriors battle the shriekers and screamers and then the lying unity. As the vision continued from where the last one left off, the beast turned to his right, where the other demons had been waiting in the wings, and he commanded, "Punishers and enforcers, join the battle!"

The new group then advanced, looking grotesque and hideous, but in a different way, their mouths huge and filled with sharp, jagged teeth. These features reminded me of deepwater fish that also have enormous mouths and sharp, pointed teeth. I somehow understood that the size and position of the demons' teeth represented different things. The longer teeth were meant to destroy the leaders of the Lion's army and dismantle the opposition from the top down. The medium-sized teeth were meant to bring intimidation, subjugation, and forced submission. The shorter teeth were meant to cause strife and division, compelling people to turn against one another. The shriekers' and screamers' power was contained in the fear and intimidation their screams caused. Lying unity possessed the power of deception through falsehood and treachery. The punishers and enforcers had power in their bite, which represented usurped authority and abusive power over others.

As the demons snaked forward, however, the Lion's army advanced toward them, unwilling to give up even an inch of holy ground. The colors around the righteous warriors changed before my eyes. Up to this point, their armor had been silver. Now all their weapons and armor were transformed into gold. In the Bible gold sometimes symbolizes God's glory, pointing to the fact that His glory has weight and value. When the armor of the righteous warriors changed color and was infused with the glory of God, the warriors became supercharged with strength and power for the battle. Then the Lion and the warriors said in unison, "You have lost. We have won! The Lion's jaws will crush the jaws of the punishers and the enforcers."

Filled with bloodlust, the punishers arrogantly enjoyed wreaking destruction. They wanted nothing more than to inflict harm and pain on those who opposed them. The enforcers, however, were more calculating. They knew they needed to subjugate their opposition and place them under false authority—a usurped authority the beast was attempting to gain and use. But the glory of God had come upon the righteous warriors, so the beast's efforts had little effect. Then the Lord's army said again, "You have lost. We have won! The Lion's jaws will crush the jaws of the punishers and the enforcers."

This time, instead of fire and light coming out of their mouths, wind came—a wind of the Spirit of God. And just as it happened with the fire and light, there were angels in the wind. The glory and the wind came together to defeat the beast's army. They were the presence of God, bringing not only refreshment and empowerment but also the answer.

I realized that I was seeing an outpouring of the Spirit of God, an outpouring of the Holy Spirit coming to the earth. It was time. During the battle I looked up and saw a clock in the heavens. It was God's clock. Time may not be an issue in the spiritual realm, but God keeps a clock in relation to His people and their physical lives, where time does matter. The impression I had was that God had planned the timing of these events and that He was now unfolding them.

The prophet Daniel spoke of God's ways in this regard:

> Blessed be the name of God forever and ever, for wisdom and might are His. And He changes the times and the seasons; He removes kings and raises up kings; He gives wisdom to the wise and knowledge to those who have understanding. He reveals deep and secret things; He knows what is in the darkness, and light dwells with Him.
>
> —DANIEL 2:20–22

In the vision of January 28, 2021, the glory and the wind came forth, and in my spirit I heard these words: "It's the wind that causes earthquakes. And earthquakes destroy strongholds. They break their foundations." I believe the Holy Spirit was saying that in addition to our third-heaven authority, God has given us weapons—fire, light, and wind—all of which are connected to His glory.

Before this vision faded, my last observations of the battlefield saw victory over the beast and his demonic hordes. I watched as the wind of the Holy Spirit increased and swirled like a tornado. As it moved across the scene, it refreshed the Lion's army but overpowered the enemy's forces. Both awe and joy filled my heart, and I sensed that this triumph would lead to a spiritual awakening on the earth.

Then came a two-and-a-half-year reprieve from the visions.

Son Light Disinfects

It was now August 6, 2023. I had been in prayer for about thirty minutes when a strong anointing of the Holy Spirit overshadowed me, and I found myself in the middle of the Lion's army once again. The entire vision played out before me as it had the last three times, and it continued to develop.

I saw the same clock in the heavens, and I witnessed the wind swirling on the battlefield. As the combat subsided, calmness spread over the scene and a light from overhead cast itself over the battlefield. I looked up and saw a sky overcast with thin clouds. I hadn't noticed it before because the battle had occurred during daylight and my focus was entirely on the fight. As I gazed upward, now two giant hands from above the overcast sky reached down and forcefully pulled the thin clouds apart, allowing a bright light to shine through the opening. The cloud separation grew wider until light bathed the entire battlefield.

By that time, most of the warfare on the battlefield had ended. Then I heard the Lion of Judah roar. Moments later the Lion's army spoke in unison with the Lion of Judah and declared, "You have lost. We have won!"

Then I heard a voice from heaven say, "Son light disinfects."

Hanging in the atmosphere in front of me appeared the words *Son Light*. Brightness and warmth from the light began spreading across the battlefield, disinfecting everything the demonic creatures had contaminated. The light was the radiance of Jesus Christ from heaven, as He declared in John 8:12, "I am the light of the world. He who follows Me shall not walk in darkness, but have the light of life." First John 3:8 adds, "He who sins is of the devil, for the devil has sinned from the beginning. For this purpose the Son of God was manifested, that He might destroy the works of the devil."

While I watched the cleansing of the battlefield, the scene changed, and I was now looking down on our nation's executive mansion, the White House. The structure was in focus directly in front of me, with the peripheral sections of Washington, DC, being dark, obscure, and not clearly visible. All focus was on the White House.

As I stared at the building, wondering what God was going to do, the same voice that said, "Son light disinfects," now decreed, "There are infections and rot in the White House. There are infections and rot in Washington, DC. There are infections and rot in American society that have allowed the rise of the demonic hordes that you warred against. The land must be disinfected."

I thought it was interesting that my wife, CK, had experienced a prophetic dream two weeks earlier in which she was in the White House. She saw the walls rotting and crumbling, with rubble falling to the floor. Those within the building did not even notice or seem to care about the spiritual collapse.

Now in the vision I heard the voice say, "Prophet, release the light."

It took me a minute to understand that the Lion was speaking to me. Surprised, I momentarily hesitated. "I'm just one of the warriors in this army," I thought. "Who am I to prophesy about that sort of thing?"

The Spirit reminded me of one other time when the Lord had addressed me as *prophet* in a vision. That time, I did what He told me to do. Now I knew the Lord had a plan and that I had better obey Him. So I fixed my gaze on the White House and then said aloud, "Release the Son light."

When I spoke, a blazing light hit the White House. Realizing the light's intensity, I looked around to see what happened, and I saw what seemed to be millions of the Lion's warriors. In synchronization they declared with me, "Release the Son light." Moved in this endeavor by the Spirit of the living God, we all spoke, "Son light, release!"

In response to our words a burst of light came from heaven and bathed the White House in its disinfectant. The light's intensity lasted for about five seconds and then let up. After about five more seconds, we said again, "Son light, release!" Again, the healing light hit the White House. This cycle repeated over and over for some time, and I felt the urgent need to persist in future prayers, intercessions, and faith decrees.

There was a distinct difference between the light that came from the mouths of the Lion's army and the disinfecting light from heaven. Both required the warriors to speak with authority. However, the light that had angels in it held warfare power, whereas the light from heaven was designed to disinfect, to heal sickness, and to make things new.

At that point, the Holy Spirit spoke to me and said, "You are one of many commanders in the Lion's army, and there are millions of warriors. Flow with Me. Move in unison. The Lord has not forgotten His covenant with those He used to establish the United States of America. He will not allow the gems of truth from holy Scripture that are contained in the nation's founding documents to be compromised by infection and rot."

Then the vision ended, and I had no choice but to obey.

Chapter 2

THE WAYS OF
THE SPIRIT

EVER SINCE THE garden, where the serpent twisted God's Word, challenged His authority, and deceived our first parents, mankind has been engaged in an epic conflict between good and evil, light and darkness. Although the fallout has caused serious ramifications in the physical realm, the battles in this war are not waged against flesh and blood; they are waged against principalities and powers in the spiritual realm (Eph. 6:12). Still, what happens in the spiritual dimension directly impacts the physical world.

The Lion's army visions pull back the curtain on the satanic plans that are playing out in the spiritual atmosphere, particularly over America. We are in a fight for our nation's continued existence, and these visions reveal some of the strategies and weapons the enemy is using to wage war. Make no mistake, the conflict must first be won in the spirit realm. Win it there, and it will be won in the hearts of American citizens and in our society and government.

The enemy is firing a barrage upon the body of Christ like never before, I believe. Why? Because we are salt and light to the world and are the conduits through which God works. The good news is that God does not leave us empty-handed. Just as the enemy has strategies and weapons, so does the Lion and His army. But these means are spiritual in nature and meant for spiritual warfare. Our weapons "are not carnal but mighty in God for pulling down strong-holds" (2 Cor. 10:4).

The church also holds the keys to the kingdom that Jesus has given us, and these keys are spiritual. Jesus said, "On this rock I will build My church, and the gates of Hades shall not prevail against it. And I will give you the keys of the kingdom of heaven, and whatever you bind on earth will be bound in heaven, and whatever you loose on earth will be loosed in heaven" (Matt. 16:18–19).

Understanding the battle is essential. In my earlier book, *Third-Heaven Authority* (which ties into this book significantly), I pointed out certain aspects of timing and of the battle lines that make warfare clearer.

> The influence the enemy was trying to exert was directed not only against the United States and many other nations, but against born-again, Spirit-filled people who might let their guard down in the spirit. The vision was a warning for us to not be deceived, but it also revealed a strategy for how to fight the warfare.
>
> One of the other things the Lord showed me concerning the vision was that the shriekers and

screamers came in after President Trump was elected to office. They came in to make noise and contest practically everything. They used violence and caused commotion. Their mission was to get attention. Their noise and intimidation tactics were meant to distract people from the real issues. They fabricated, misconstrued, and attacked. They released anger, hatred, and character assassination, and it's still going on today.

The second army, lying unity, came before the 2020 US presidential election. Again, they were attempting to deceive people and cause them to feel like they had to surrender. They had to project unity, but it was a false, fleshly unity. It wasn't wisdom from the Spirit of God. It was the enemy attempting to control people and cause those who were not part of their so-called unity to look like rebellious fools and be mocked as extremists.

The demonic warriors in lying unity reeked of contempt and deceit. "Oh, let's trick them," they must have said. "Let's pull the wool over their eyes, and everything will be fine. We'll bring peace on all sides. We're here to save the day." They are still working their deception today.

The third demonic army was made up of the punishers and enforcers. They came on the heels of lying unity, but just before Biden's January 2021 inauguration. Quickly they set out to chastise and force everybody to come in line with them, or else. They intended to rule the day.[1]

In chapter 1, I mentioned the deployment of the Lion's army to disinfect the White House. That deployment seemed to commence in the middle of 2023 and to strengthen in 2024. The sheer fact that I saw the White House in need of disinfectant points to how effective the demonic hordes had been. Their ungodly influence was apparent in a society where multitudes rejected Jesus and possessed either no moral compass or a warped moral compass that calls "evil good, and good evil" (Isa. 5:20). Therefore, people became prey to deceptive spirits and the perverted ideologies that such spirits espouse. Even Christians were deceived. Many who faltered were believers who were biblically illiterate or who tried to live their faith through emotionalism and people-pleasing.

Weapons from God

In *Third-Heaven Authority* I wrote the following about three weapons that the Lion's army used: spiritual power and authority, light, and wind.

In some ways, to the undiscerning public these three armies looked legit. They seemed reasonable on the outside, but deep inside they were vile, wicked, contemptuous antichrist spirits. The Lord, on the other hand, gave weapons to the righteous army.

The first weapon against the shriekers and the screamers was the fire in the mouths of the believers. It was spiritual power and authority. In the spiritual realm, it's the ability to bind and cut off the lies of the advancing horde. It was a weapon in their mouths, symbolizing how as we decree, we by faith release authority into the spiritual atmosphere. The second weapon in the mouths of the righteous army was light. This represents spiritual truth and discernment. And the third weapon was wind, which is the outpouring of the Holy Spirit and God's glory coming forth on the face of the earth.

We are the warriors. We have Jesus inside us as well as the power of His blood along with the right to use His name. There is power in our mouths. Jesus said of Himself, "All authority has been given to Me in heaven and on earth" (Matt. 28:18). That means the body of Christ is releasing authority from heaven itself onto the earth. We don't go forward as lambs but as warriors carrying the sword of justice and righteousness. It is our job to stand against that onslaught from the Far Left. And we do so as the righteous army. We say to the shriekers and screamers, "You have lost; we have won." We say to lying unity and its deception, "You have lost; we have won." We say to the punishers and enforcers, "You have lost; we have won!"[2]

And we say to the White House, "Son light, release!"

Another thing the Lord showed me is that Satan's strategies are free-floating and cyclical. The word *free-floating* means that there are demonic spirits behind his strategies and that the activity is not associated with any one event. Like a swarm of flies, demons hover, always looking to attach themselves to any passing event or situation that will host their influence. The goal is to cause disruption, deception, and punishment, as well as to control. They hate Jesus and His church, and they hate the United States and Israel.

In addition to the main cycle of demonic attacks that I've already described, we see the same cycle repeating over and over again. First come the shriekers and screamers, followed by the lying unity, which gives way to the punishers and enforcers. We witnessed this cycle in Donald Trump's presidential term and in Justice Brett Kavanaugh's hearings when he was nominated for and confirmed into the US Supreme Court. We witnessed it in the Black Lives Matter riots during the mislabeled Summer of Love. We witnessed it when the US Supreme Court overturned *Roe v. Wade*. And as I'm writing this, we are witnessing it in anti-Israel, anti-Semitic protests.

Apart from some changing of character roles, pretty much the same people were involved in each uprising. Once you identify the demonic cycle, it becomes easier to identify its operation in recurring events. You can also witness it on a more personal level that concerns situations within your own family, work environment, or community. Armed with this knowledge, you can confront the cycle immediately, using the spiritual weapons that God provides.

It's time to refuse intimidation and take a stand.

THE WAYS OF THE SPIRIT

One day while I was talking to the Lord in prayer, He spoke to me and said, "I want you to teach the ways of the Spirit to My people for these last days. It is imperative for the Lion's army to understand how the spiritual realm works. All believers must know how to live a Spirit-filled life."

When the Lord gave me this instruction, I realized how large the task was. I had spent more than four decades learning what I knew about the ways of the Spirit. Every revelation I gleaned came from the Word of God, real-life experience, and spiritual encounters. Always, the Word of God is the plumb line of truth. So whatever I experience or encounter I hold up to the Scriptures and measure it from that perspective.

The overall purpose of this book is to teach believers how to live effective, fulfilling, Spirit-filled lives by understanding the ways of the Spirit. My visions of the Lion's army illustrate how real the spirit realm and the spiritual battle are. As human beings we live and operate in both the spiritual and physical realms. Therefore, we will explore the following aspects of a Spirit-filled life:

- walking in the Spirit, step by step
- our spiritual creation and makeup
- the gifts of the Spirit
- hearing the voice of God
- praying in the Spirit
- visions and dreams
- performing miracles
- faith and spiritual authority
- revival and spiritual awakening
- successful spiritual warfare

David, the king and psalmist, placed great importance on understanding the Lord's ways and how they would lead him into the Lord's paths. David penned the words, "Show me Your ways, O LORD; teach me Your paths" (Ps. 25:4). The prophet Isaiah also spoke along these lines, writing, "For as the heavens are higher than the earth, so are My ways higher than your ways, and My thoughts than your thoughts" (Isa. 55:9).

Three takeaways from Isaiah 55:9 immediately come to mind.

1. There are the ways of the Lord, which are spiritual, and there are the ways of man, which are natural.

2. God's ways are perfect and aligned with all creation. They reveal His purposes for a redeemed humanity. Since He is the manufacturer (so to speak), His manufacturer's handbook (the Bible) discloses the full operating capabilities of our lives. Man's ways, which fall woefully short of our potential, are focused on fallen nature and worldly knowledge.

3. Although God's ways are higher, they remain discoverable. We can learn the ways of the Lord and be called up into His way of thinking and living.

David would have agreed with Isaiah's third point, as David's words in Psalm 103:7 show that "He [God] made known His ways to Moses, His acts to the children of Israel." The ways of the Lord produce the acts of the Lord. It behooves us to learn the ways of the Lord so we can move according to His will, purpose, power, and direction in our lives.

In talking about the Lord's ways, it is vital to understand the Lord is one God in three distinct persons. The Trinity, or Godhead, consists of God the Father, God the Son, and God the Holy Spirit. That may seem elementary to you, but it's important to know the distinct role each person of the Godhead plays. When the Lord told me to teach the ways of the Spirit, I understood Him to mean that my teachings on how the spiritual realm functions should concentrate on how the person of the Holy Spirit operates.

So let's talk about *ways.* The words often translated "ways" in Scripture are *derek* in Hebrew and *hodos* in Greek. Each term refers to a "road" or "path."[3] To travel the road of His ways requires a course of thinking and a mode of action. In other words, it involves how the Holy Spirit thinks, plans, and then moves in our lives.

Notice what Paul wrote: "If we live in the Spirit, let us also walk in the Spirit" (Gal. 5:25). Everything that pertains to life and godliness is found in the Spirit, so we should walk in line with the Holy Spirit's leading, step by step, turn by turn, revelation by revelation, and empowerment by empowerment. The Holy Spirit is our spiritual GPS, revealing the best path to follow. However, we must be connected with Him to receive His signal and power. Jesus spoke of this connection, saying, "I am the vine, you are the branches. He who abides in Me, and I in him, bears much fruit; for without Me you can do nothing" (John 15:5).

When Paul addressed the Corinthian church concerning spiritual gifts, he explained that the ways of the Holy Spirit could be adapted to a person's individual gift mix of personality, talents, ministry, and so forth (1 Cor. 12:4–6). Then Paul said, "But the manifestation of the Spirit is given to each one for the profit of all" (1 Cor. 12:7). The ways of the Spirit find manifestation and expression by revealing themselves openly in your life. Their effect is physically detectable within your environment. That's why I said the ways of the Spirit produce the acts of the Spirit. These manifestations are for *each one*, and that includes you.

ARE WE IN THE LAST DAYS?

When the Lord told me to teach the ways of the Spirit for the last days, I was surprised and several questions arose in my mind. I had a pretty good grasp on what the Scriptures say about the last days, and I realized that most people associate them purely with the return of the Lord and many tribulation-type events. However, much confusion surrounds these prophetic matters.

My visions of the Lion's army revealed the demonic wickedness behind a host of troubling things happening in the United States and the world. The escalation of Marxism, Communism, socialism, atheism, and militant Islam is ripping apart the fabric of our country. Add to that deviant sexual beliefs, gender distortion, trans activism, and surgical mutilation of children's bodies to affirm their emotional confusions.

Instead of believing all people are created equal in the sight of God, race politics and diversity, equity, and inclusion (DEI) have caused unparalleled division. Meanwhile, we are seeing the most intense persecution of Christians and Jews in several generations. Mix all these elements together, and you have a level of cultural insanity and confusion that leads to hopelessness and despair.

In such an environment it's easy to assume that these are the days preceding the Lord's return. Because of this some believers have given themselves over to fear. Some become silent and inactive in their faith. They succumb to the false notion that things will only get worse and there is nothing they can do. "Why even try?" they ask, as though spiritual laws don't even work anymore. At the same time, other believers become more zealous in their soul winning, wanting to take as many people to heaven with them as they can, while they still can.

Once again, I inquired of the Lord, and He dropped His answer into my spirit: "As we get closer to My return, the ways of the Holy Spirit will not change. They remain consistent through all the ages."

There was the key! I now knew what the Lord was asking of me, and I knew what to pursue. Let me explain. In the Bible, Jewish teachers divided time into two basic parts. The first is the former time, which consisted of everything before and leading up to the appearance of the Messiah. The last days are the second part; they began during the time of the Messiah and include the future prophetic times and events that will occur with the second coming of Jesus. We have been living in the last days for over two thousand years.

We typically recognize time in terms of the Old and New Testaments. This is illustrated by the writer to the Hebrews, who wrote, "God, who at various times and in various ways spoke in time past to the fathers by the prophets, has in these last days spoken to us by His Son, whom He has appointed heir of all things, through whom also He made the worlds" (Heb. 1:1–2). Of course *His Son*, Jesus Christ, is the Messiah, whose appearance and message triggered the last days. The last days include the time of salvation, or what we call the church age.

They began with Jesus' birth but were fully revealed during the outpouring of the Holy Spirit on the day of Pentecost. The last days will continue until the second return of the Lord. Luke covered this idea.

But this is what was spoken by the prophet Joel: "And it shall come to pass in the last days, says God, that I will pour out of My Spirit on all flesh; your sons and your daughters shall prophesy, your young men shall see visions, your old men shall dream dreams. And on My menservants and on My maidservants I will pour out My Spirit in those days; and they shall prophesy. I will show wonders in heaven above and signs in the earth beneath: blood and fire and vapor of smoke. The sun shall be turned into darkness, and the moon into blood, before the coming of the great and awesome day of the LORD. And it shall come to pass that whoever calls on the name of the LORD shall be saved."

—ACTS 2:16–21

This means that everyone who was alive during the original day of Pentecost and everyone who was born since then has lived (or is living) in the last days. It also means that the Holy Spirit has been given to manifest His ways, which have been consistent during the entire span of these last days.

Technically, we are living in the last days now. You may ask, "Aren't things going to get worse as we get closer to the Lord's return?" Paul did indicate that this is probably true.

But know this, that in the last days perilous times will come: for men will be lovers of themselves, lovers of money, boasters, proud, blasphemers, disobedient to parents, unthankful, unholy, unloving, unforgiving, slanderers, without self-control, brutal, despisers of good, traitors, headstrong, haughty, lovers of pleasure rather than lovers of God, having a form of godliness but denying its power. And from such people turn away!

—2 TIMOTHY 3:1–5

Paul also wrote, "Now the Spirit expressly says that in latter times some will depart from the faith, giving heed to deceiving spirits and doctrines of demons" (1 Tim. 4:1). He knew that during the entire span of the last days, some people would be blasphemous lovers of themselves. However, in this case he seems to be referring to the last days of the last days.

Peter also picked up on the theme of the last days by warning "that scoffers will come in the last days, walking according to their own lusts" (2 Pet. 3:3). Both Paul and Peter heard prophetic warnings from the Holy Spirit and foretold what were still future events to them. Peter wrapped up that portion of his second letter by writing, "But the day of the Lord will come as a thief in the night" (2 Pet. 3:10).

Yes, things will get worse before the Lord's return, but His return "will come as a thief in the night," meaning no one knows when it will happen. Matthew touched on the timing of Jesus' return when he wrote that Jesus said, "Watch therefore, for you know neither the day nor the hour in which the Son of Man is coming" (Matt. 25:13). The Lord would have us focus on learning the ways of the Spirit rather than the evil in the world. We see what Satan is doing around us, but we need to also see what Jesus is doing through His church. At no point will the Lion's army be powerless. God has raised a fighting force to meet the demonic challenges of this day, and His army will only become larger and better trained in the days ahead.

I want to close this chapter with two final points. First,

we don't know which tribulation of these last days will precede the Lord's return. No one knows the day or the hour, and hard times don't necessarily point to anything other than Satan working wickedness in humanity. My good friend and late Messianic rabbi Rich Ford said something to me years ago that affected my thinking. He said there is a difference between how Gentile Christians and Jewish Christians view the trials of the last days. Gentile believers try to judge whether Jesus is coming back by how difficult the times seem. Jewish believers don't do this because Jewish people have suffered so much throughout history. Dr. Ford said that Messianic survivors of Hitler's death camps during WWII couldn't fathom anything being worse. If the Holocaust wasn't the sign of Christ's imminent return, then Christians need to quit looking for the end of the world and instead stand against the evil of the day. The Lord will return when the Father tells Him to return.

My second point is that the ways of the Spirit will not change or diminish as the Lord's return draws closer. Spiritual laws remain constant. The power in the church will stay the same as it continues to be the light of the world and the salt of the earth. Because we serve Him and trust His design for our future, the mysteries of God will keep unfolding before us.

Our attitude then is one of faith and authority. Regardless of the world's ups and downs, following the ways of the Spirit will provide the best life possible—and it will empower us to continue the fight against evil until the hour of Jesus' return.

Chapter 3

MORE LION'S ARMY VISIONS

O VER THE PAST few years, the Holy Spirit has given me additional visions relating to my original Lion's army vision. I believe they were designed to reveal deeper insights about what God is doing behind the scenes. They also keep me alert to the spiritual warfare in which we are engaged. My purpose in sharing these supplementary visions is that you too may glean deeper revelation from the Spirit of God.

IDOL SPIRITS OF OLD

On November 18, 2021, while worshipping the Lord and praying in other tongues, I heard the faint rumblings of a Lion roaring in the distance. Upon hearing the sound, an anointing flooded my being, and the Holy Spirit pulled me into the spiritual realm. The roars continued in the other dimension, one after another, thundering more loudly each time. Looking down from the elevated position that the vision provided, I could see that the roars were coming from the same colossal Lion I had seen before.

As I did previously, I instinctively knew that this was Jesus, the Lion of Judah. Within His atmosphere-shaking roars the words "You have lost. We have won!" again sounded. He was speaking and decreeing directly to the enemy, Satan himself, and to his legions of demonic cronies. The Lion was giving them notice.

Also as before, stretched out in front of the Lion were thousands upon thousands of His righteous warriors. They were born-again men and women, including you and me, who had picked up the mantle of the army of God to war in His name and walk in their rightful authority. They were putting down the enemy while building up God's kingdom. As the Lion's roars and words entered into the backs of these warriors, they declared in unison with their leader, "You have lost. We have won!" The words shot forth from their mouths as spiritual vibrations that became rolling sound waves of power.

Standing in front of the righteous army in a half-circle formation were about twenty or so tall, statue-like idols made of wood, stone, gold, and other inanimate materials. Strangely, the face of a demon appeared on the face of each idol. Although the idols were not made of living materials, each had a living face peeking out from its head. My mind instantly went to 1 Corinthians 10:20, where the apostle Paul told new Gentile believers that sacrificing to idols meant sacrificing to demons (the enticing influences and spiritual powers behind idolatry) rather than God.

Looking into the faces of the idols, I discerned that they were ancient spirits that had been lurking for thousands of years and were now reinserting themselves into present societies and cultures. As this understanding came to me, the idol spirits spoke. "Civilizations throughout time have worshipped us," they snarled and sneered. "America and the nations of the earth will bow before us again."

I couldn't determine who all the spirits were, but I sensed the presence of Baal manifesting as a Jezebel spirit in America. Two things were certain: they were all anti-christ in nature, and all were highly seductive. Yet no sooner had they spoken than the sound waves hit them, the sound waves from the vibrating words of the Lion's army, shattering the statues and their control and deception.

It was then that the righteous warriors shifted from speaking in a single voice to speaking in their individual languages. Still, they remained curiously in sync as one army. Although a variety of heavenly languages were being spoken, by the Spirit I could discern at least five distinct types.

1. One was the language of warfare, with warriors binding, loosing, and confronting various evil spirits. The authority in their voices was palpable as they spoke of strategies for future battles.

2. Simultaneously, I heard languages of worship and praise being offered unto the Lion, who could destroy the enemy's works. Songs filled the atmosphere and soothed it with the fragrances of hope and power.

3. The third type of language was one of creativity for building God's kingdom. Its words were constructing destinies and

speaking divine plans that brought into manifestation righteousness, deliverance, healing, and salvation.

4. The fourth type was angelic languages communicating with and helping the warriors in the tasks the Lion had assigned them. The angels engaged in building the kingdom and the destinies of God's children on the earth.

5. The fifth type involved languages of the Word. The righteous warriors spoke the Word of God in various dialects, reciting extensive portions of Scripture. Curiously, the Word came out of their mouths as a living presence. The Lion's army launched God's Word into the atmosphere with its self-fulfilling power to accomplish what was spoken.

While pondering these things, I heard the voice of the Lion asking, "Who can stand against me?" Then He declared, "All will fall before the terrible presence of the Lord. And that presence is in the hearts and mouths of My warriors. My army shall do valiantly. There is a time coming when evil will be put down, but until that time, My army shall resist it."

The Lord showed me the intensity of the battle for America. We can define many fronts where unrighteousness has increased in our nation. However, the Lord defined idolatry as the major one. We are a nation of idols. The good news is that the vision contained the prophetic promise that the Lion's army can cause the idols' influence to crumble. Remember, you cannot kill a spirit, but you can exercise authority over it and diminish its control.

THE STRONG LION AND THE WEAK LION

Earlier, near the fall of 2021 on August 22, a Sunday afternoon, another vision came right in the middle of my sermon. The spirit realm opened before me as the Holy Spirit drew me in to watch the vision unfold. The setting was the side of a rolling hill peppered with brush, rocks, and trees. At the base of the hill, open meadows spread out into rural farmlands and small communities. Beyond them I could see the surrounding cities.

The hill was not very steep. On the lower part of its incline, a lion lifted its head and roared. As I looked more closely, this lion seemed weak, gaunt, and dirty, and his mane was scraggly. While hunting and on the prowl, his roar was intended to produce fear, but it was unconvincing and lacked power. Despite his appearance, a sly arrogance seemed to seep from him, as though he was unaware of his pathetic condition. He was neither a young lion nor a decrepit one. He seemed to simply be an ancient beast that had feasted on numerous types of prey in the past.

Then movement higher up on the hill caught my attention. There stood a magnificent Lion, large and regal, with a full mane and shimmering coat that highlighted His confident way of carrying Himself. There was an indescribable depth in His eyes. His muscles were finely developed. And when He roared, the sound was both thunderous and fierce. Obviously, this was the Lion of Judah, Jesus Christ, which could only mean that the weak lion was Satan.

Startled by the strong Lion's deafening roar, the weak

lion shook with fear and scurried into hiding. The strong Lion roared again, and the words in His thunder were the same as before: "You have lost. We have won!"

The Lion's roar reverberated throughout the countryside, echoing in the surrounding mountains and canyons. This time, however, a rainbow glory cloud appeared around Him and began expanding and rolling down the hill. The cloud contained a swirling mix of bright colors, just as the rainbow glory did that I saw in heaven's throne room during a supernatural encounter I describe in my book *Third-Heaven Authority*.[1] It was the rainbow glory that emanates from God Himself.

In the August 2021 vision, I heard an angel saying, "The seven Spirits of God that are before the throne release a glorious anointing." I recognized John's use of the term *seven Spirits* in referring to the Holy Spirit in Revelation 1:4—"John, to the seven churches which are in Asia: Grace to you and peace from Him who is and who was and who is to come, and from the seven Spirits who are before His throne."

What I witnessed was an outpouring of the Holy Spirit and of God's glory on the earth. The rainbow cloud flowed down the hillside and across the farms, ranches, and rural communities. It kept moving to the cities, where it flowed down every street and touched people as it expanded. Many were oblivious to its presence, but those who felt it responded by inhaling deeply. When they did, they sucked the cloud into their lungs, and it transformed them. They were born again and filled with the Spirit of God. Miracles began to happen. Healings manifested in their bodies and in their relationships. Hearts were changed, families were restored, and great joy came upon them as they worshipped the Lion. Several angels declared, "Even creation itself is waiting for the manifestation of the Son of God. And the knowledge of the glory of the Lord will fill the earth. The nations will bow before the Lion."

Then the vision faded away.

THE YOUNG LIONS

During our Sunday afternoon service on March 12, 2023, it happened again—another open vision. This time, however, it started during worship while my son Bryan led us in heavenly praise. The anointing was heavy in the room as I found myself back on the same hillside that I saw in the vision of the strong Lion and the weak lion.

The weak lion was still in hiding at this point and was nowhere to be seen. However, there stood the Lion of Judah, in all His regal form, who had just released the rainbow cloud of glory. Lifting His head, He roared, and as it always did, His roar carried within it the words "You have lost. We have won!"

When those words came out this time, something occurred that I had not seen in any previous visions. An innumerable number of younger lions appeared around the Lion of Judah. A sense of His awesomeness—of being strong, healthy, and eager—was upon them. They had His DNA, which contained His values and purposes. He was the strong Lion, and they were His pride, His army of young lions. I realized that these young lions represented believers who were born of the Spirit of God, and this scripture came to mind: "For whom He foreknew, He also predestined to be conformed to the image of His Son, that He might be the firstborn among many brethren" (Rom. 8:29).

All at once, the young lions ran down the hill to fulfill

an important mission. They followed the same path that the glory cloud had taken in my previous vision, and as they moved, the glory surrounded them. They were running with the glory! The Spirit of God was in these young lions, and the glory was upon them. Wherever the Spirit and the glory went, the young lions went. The Spirit within them was their Guide, and the glory upon them was their empowerment.

As they ran, some young lions split off individually or in pairs to go to specific farms or rural homes. Groups of between three and ten young lions broke away to enter small communities. Larger groups ran toward the larger cities. Regardless of a destination's size or population, the young lions followed the path of God's glory and went wherever people were.

All this time, the weak lion remained in hiding. He hated the glory and the young lions who spread it. For a long period of time, he actively set up and developed his opposition to the glory. But the strong Lion had given to the young lions authority to overcome the opposition. They were like the warriors in my original vision. They worked harmoniously with God's glory, and when they roared at the adversary in whatever form, the adversary would crumble and fall.

What's interesting is that the young lions did more than battle evil forces; they were also intercessors, evangelists, and miracle workers carrying the life-filling glory of God. They had spiritual faith and authority that demonstrated the Great Commission and its ability to save the lost by overcoming Satan's strongholds.

And He [Jesus] said to them, "Go into all the world and preach the gospel to every creature. He who believes and is baptized will be saved; but he who does not believe will be condemned. And these signs will follow those who believe: In My name they will cast out demons; they will speak with new tongues; they will take up serpents; and if they drink anything deadly, it will by no means hurt them; they will lay hands on the sick, and they will recover."

So then, after the Lord had spoken to them, He was received up into heaven, and sat down at the right hand of God. And they went out and preached everywhere, the Lord working with them and confirming the word through the accompanying signs. Amen.

—Mark 16:15–20

The vision ended.

❧

The vision of March 12, 2023, was a vision of an army of lions rather than a vision of the Lion's army.

What's the difference? The other Lion's army visions were about warfare itself. They unveiled the strategies and weapons Satan uses against our nation behind the seen realm. They revealed the powerful weapons believers must use in warfare—specifically "the weapons of our warfare [that] are not carnal but mighty in God for pulling down strongholds" (2 Cor. 10:4).

The March 2023 vision of the army of lions emphasized the outpouring of the Holy Spirit. The body of Christ has

Christ's DNA, which allows us to work with and carry God's glory for the sake of revival and spiritual awakening. We are believers and new creations in Christ Jesus—are we not? "Therefore, if anyone is in Christ, he is a new creation; old things have passed away; behold, all things have become new" (2 Cor. 5:17).

Dear reader, God is unfolding His divine plans in these last days. We are part of His plans. Therefore, it is critically important that we come to the full revelation of (1) who He created us to be in Jesus Christ and (2) what is available to us through Him.

My purpose in the remainder of this book is to reveal the beauty of the Spirit's ways so each of us can fulfill our destinies in Jesus. I pray for you in the name of Jesus Christ that the anointing that is upon these visions will be released into your life. I pray that the Spirit of revelation will ignite a fire within all our hearts and make us valiant and effective warriors of Christ's kingdom.

Let us cry out together in faith to God, "Our Father in heaven, hallowed be Your name. Your kingdom come. Your will be done on earth as it is in heaven" (Matt. 6:9–10).

Chapter 4

UNDERSTANDING THE SPIRITUAL REALM

EING RAISED SOUTHERN Baptist, growing up I knew the Bible talks a lot about heaven and hell. I wanted to go to heaven, so I accepted Jesus as my Savior. I went to church faithfully. I could quote John 3:16 and explain the plan of salvation with the best of them. I'll always be indebted to my Baptist brethren for leading me to Jesus, but I had zero understanding of the spiritual realm or spiritual warfare or what it means to walk in the Spirit.

The thing is, what happens in the spiritual realm directly impacts the physical realm. I didn't know this and was trying my best to live the Christian life in my own power. It wasn't working, and my soul knew there had to be more. Unfortunately, much of the church lives that way. They know there's a spiritual realm of light and darkness, and they believe that when they die, they will go to a very real heaven. However, they function in the here and now as though the Holy Spirit were irrelevant and the spiritual realm didn't exist. As a result, they lack power. They live in frustration, or even worse, in spiritual lethargy, allowing the enemy to run roughshod over them and their circles of influence.

Fortunately, there is more for those who want all that God has for them and are willing to learn. It wasn't until I was baptized in the Holy Spirit and had immersed myself in studying God's Word on the subject that the spiritual realm really opened up to me. I became a spiritual sponge, absorbing the teachings of anointed men and women of God who knew much more about walking in the Spirit than I did.

Over the years, the Holy Spirit faithfully guided my understanding, line upon line and precept upon precept (Isa. 28:10), until walking in the Spirit became a way of life. I often tell people it's similar to walking with one foot in the spiritual realm and one foot in the physical realm. As I continue walking, the Lord graces me with countless spiritual encounters, none of which are prompted by me. They are sovereign acts that leave me humbled, in awe, and feeling the weight of the responsibility they carry. Within each one, I have witnessed spiritual dynamics and biblical principles that I can pass on to you for application in your life and calling.

This Lion's army consists of untold numbers of righteous warriors, individuals like you and me, each with a unique and necessary role to play. Now, let's examine some of the dynamics and biblical principles concerning the spiritual realm.

Two Distinct Realms

One foundational truth to understand is that there are two distinct realms of existence and influence. The Bible reveals them as the spiritual realm and the physical realm, also known as the supernatural and the natural. This may seem elementary, but trust me, it's critical. These realms are distinct and radically different from one another, yet they overlap. And always remember that you have influence in whichever realm you occupy.

In the first couple of chapters of Genesis we read how God (who is Spirit, according to John 4:24) created the celestial heavens and the earth. The physical realm was specifically fashioned as a living environment for mankind. God encapsulated this idea when He spoke the following words to the prophet Isaiah: "For thus says the Lord, who created the heavens, who is God, who formed the earth and made it, who has established it, who did not create it in vain, *who formed it to be inhabited*: 'I am the Lord, and there is no other'" (Isa. 45:18).

Simply put, God established physical time, space, and matter—the dimensions of the physical realm—to form a habitation for the special beings He created in His own image. These dimensions did not exist before creation, even though God and the spiritual realm already existed at that time. He formed the laws of physics, but He is not bound by them. The dimensions in the spiritual realm exist outside the physical. Thus, spiritual dimensions are governed by separate laws in which time, space, and matter do not exercise control. Past, present, and future are absorbed into eternity.

Consider Ezekiel's wheel within a wheel. In Ezekiel

chapter 1 the prophet used an illustration of a chariot to describe God's throne. He was grasping for words because the chariot, or throne, stretches from heaven to earth, allowing God to see in all directions and travel in all directions at the same time. In the natural realm this is impossible. But why does Ezekiel describe God's throne this way? And how is it possible?

Obviously, it is possible because God is God, but it's also possible because He's of the spiritual realm. Think of the wheel as a sphere. In the natural realm, we have bicycle wheels. Each wheel has a tire plus a central hub and outer rim connected by spokes. To change directions, the bicycle tire must be turned in a new direction. Also, according to natural laws, the only way to put one wheel inside another wheel is for them to be different sizes.

In the Spirit, however, Ezekiel described God's chariot as having multiple wheels. He wrote, "This was the appearance and structure of the wheels: They sparkled like topaz, and all four looked alike. Each appeared to be made like a wheel intersecting a wheel" (Ezek. 1:16, NIV). The intersecting wheels were the same size and pointed in different directions, making them appear as spheres that could go in any direction without changing course. "As they moved, they would go in any one of the four directions the creatures faced; the wheels did not change direction as the creatures went" (Ezek. 1:17, NIV). I like to think of God being in the hub and possessing the ability to simultaneously look through all the spokes. All at the same time, He views what we call past, present, and future in both the physical and spiritual realms, and He can move His throne in all directions without turning.

Has your mind turned to mush yet? The prophet did his

best to describe how spiritual laws are, but I'm sure he felt as if his words fell short. Nevertheless, he obeyed and, to the best of his ability, reported what he saw. Addressing the Holy Spirit's involvement, Ezekiel wrote, "Wherever the spirit would go, they would go, and the wheels would rise along with them, because the spirit of the living creatures was in the wheels" (Ezek. 1:20, NIV).

Even though God created His children to inhabit the realm where physical time, space, and matter exist, He also designed us to coexist with the spiritual realm. Adam and Eve lived in that coexistence until the fall created a break. As a result, we must now be reconciled back through the second Adam, Jesus, and then learn how to operate in the Spirit without being limited by our natural bodies. Therefore, we embrace our natural lives but subjugate them to the spiritual laws of God's kingdom.

God's spiritual kingdom is the parent of the physical realm. Hebrews 11:3 says, "By faith we understand that the universe was formed at God's command, so that what is seen was not made out of what was visible" (NIV). Since the parent realm gave birth to the child realm, the spiritual has authority over the physical. In other words, the things of the Spirit affect the things of the physical realm. Throughout the pages of Scripture we see spiritual laws overriding natural laws.

On the negative side of the equation, Satan and demons wield an evil influence on the physical realm and the people inhabiting it. The Lion's army visions illustrate this point, and the Bible shows us that sin, sickness, and poverty on earth are direct results of Satan's spiritual perversion. However, on the positive side, the Holy Spirit uses spiritual truth and power for our redemption, because "the law of the Spirit of life in Christ Jesus has made [us] free from the law of sin and death" (Rom. 8:2).

Spiritual things are both constant and eternal. They have greater significance than the ever-changing physical things in our lives. Therefore, Paul wrote, "We do not look at the things which are seen, but at the things which are not seen. For the things which are seen are temporary, but the things which are not seen are eternal" (2 Cor. 4:18).

This is a hard truth to grasp, even for believers—especially for those whose focus is primarily on the natural world and what it offers. Yet the truth that the spirit realm is more real than the physical one is at the core of everything we are learning here. The spiritual realm is more real not because the physical realm is an illusion; the spiritual realm is more real because it has the power to alter the physical realm. To begin with, God, who is outside time, space, and matter, created the physical universe. The unseen created the seen; the Spirit formed the natural. Therefore, the natural is subject to the laws of the Spirit.

As believers we must awaken to this realization and understand that our ability to change things in the natural realm is only possible through the spiritual realm. The spirit parts of us work to change the things that the physical parts of us cannot. When a doctor diagnoses a disease and pronounces it incurable, he or she is admitting that neither natural man nor scientific knowledge are yet able to alter that physical fact. This restriction does not hold up in the Spirit, however. Again, Jesus said, "They will lay hands on the sick, and they will recover" (Mark 16:18). So according to Jesus, spiritual law supersedes natural law and changes it. Everything around you is subject to the spiritual realm.

CREATED TO EXIST IN BOTH
REALMS SIMULTANEOUSLY

As I already pointed out, mankind was created by God to simultaneously exist in both worlds. Our physical bodies were formed from the earth, but they are kept alive by our spirits, which are inside us. In reality our bodies are earth suits that allow our spirits to function in this realm.

When God created Adam, what did He do? First, He made Adam's body. Then He placed Adam's spiritual being within his body. Specifically, "The LORD God formed man of the dust of the ground, and breathed into his nostrils the breath of life; and man became a living being" (Gen. 2:7). Without the breath of life Adam's body never would have been animated. Therefore, it's been said that we are not physical beings having a spiritual experience; rather, we are spiritual beings having a physical experience.

Because we are spiritual beings, there is no small discussion in the body of Christ over how God influences us. Some believe that our relationship with Him is only contemplative, meaning that He speaks through the Bible and then occupies our minds, impressing His will upon our thoughts to lead and guide us. This is the basic approach taken by the part of the church that doesn't practice Spirit baptism with Charismatic manifestations.

Those believers who are Spirit filled and have a Charismatic lifestyle also believe that the Bible is the final authority and that God influences the corporeal parts of who we are. But Spirit-filled people believe there can also be ecstatic feelings of the Holy Spirit's presence within and upon us. We call these feelings the glory of God and Spirit anointing.

I am in this camp of people and can attest that our physical bodies can feel the spiritual presence of God, as well as the effects of the Holy Spirit upon us. There are tangible anointings on our bodies. We can be slain in the Spirit (falling) when the body is not able to continue standing because of the overwhelming presence of the Spirit. We can experience trances in which the physical senses are suspended for a time so the Spirit can impress a vision upon our spiritual senses. These are just a few illustrations of how the Spirit affects us bodily.

I'm reminded of the first word of knowledge that I received from the Lord. CK and I had just surrendered to our call to ministry. We had been married only a few years, and I was scheduled to go to Bible school that fall. Our pastor asked me to preach some Wednesday night services for him and fill in as a teacher for a home Bible study. While I was praying and preparing for the home meeting one night, I kept getting a weird feeling in my right elbow. It started tingling, almost as if I had hit my funny bone. What is strange and hard to articulate is that the feeling wasn't physical. I felt it in the spiritual sense, yet it touched my body.

At that point in my walk, I had learned some things by watching other men and women of God operating in the gifts of the Spirit. I knew just enough to think that I may have been getting a word of knowledge. I filed the experience in the back of my mind and taught the Bible study that night. After the teaching, I closed my Bible—and the sensation in my elbow returned.

With all the faith I could muster, I said, "Hey, I've never done this before, but I keep feeling this weird tingling right here in my elbow. Has anyone here been having a problem with their right elbow?"

Immediately, a hand shot up across the room, and its owner said, "It's me! My elbow has been killing me. I'm a piano tuner, and I've been cranking keys all day long." Then he said, "Wait a minute—it's gone. The moment I raised my hand, the pain completely left. God just healed it. Thank You, Jesus!"

That was a learning experience for me, and it taught me to pay attention to manifestations. Have you ever felt an uncontrollable unction to laugh out loud or cry under an anointing? Those kinds of manifestations are important. God moves upon us not only to bless us but to make us conduits of blessing to others. As Jesus and His apostles did, we also must learn to allow spiritual power and authority to flow through us.

THE SPIRITUAL AFFECTS THE PHYSICAL

Remember that the spiritual realm affects the corporeal realm. Once you are born again and the spirit within you comes alive, it operates in the spiritual realm while your body continues to function in the physical one. As John wrote, "That which is born of the flesh is flesh, and that which is born of the Spirit is spirit" (John 3:6). I'll talk more about this later, but for now I'll say that our minds can bridge these two realms. Paul wrote, "And do not be conformed to this world, but be transformed by the renewing of your mind" (Rom. 12:2). Notice that *conforming* to the world happens naturally, because we live in this natural world. However, *transformation*, which is spiritual and supernatural, requires our minds to be

49

renewed. The mind is like a bridge; therefore, we can live in that transformed, supernatural state.

Similarly, the altering of natural laws can change physical circumstances. For example, "when Paul had gathered a bundle of sticks and laid them on the fire, a viper came out because of the heat, and fastened on his hand" (Acts 28:3). This event could have been fatal, "but he shook off the creature into the fire and suffered no harm" (Acts 28:5).

That was a miracle! A poisonous snake took its fangs and latched on to Paul, yet he didn't die. Why? The witnesses expected him to keel over, but he didn't. It was as though nothing had happened. God used that miracle to capture the attention of Paul's former shipmates and the people of Malta so Paul could preach Jesus to them. (See Acts 27:39–28:10.) Someone who operates purely out of their intellect might say, "Well, you know, Paul was gathering sticks. So the viper probably struck at the sticks and released its lethal venom before attaching itself to Paul's hand."

That might be considered a brilliant conclusion for a tenured professor at certain theological institutions, but it would only force the things of God into a physical, mental framework. It's important that we reason with the Lord's kind of reasoning and not man's. To understand and operate in spiritual things, we must use spiritual reasoning that comes from having the mind of Christ.

Consider the account in John chapter 2 of Jesus turning water into wine at a wedding celebration. How do you rationally explain away that miracle? You can't unless you say, "He did it because He is God and we're not. So we can't do what He did." But if that were true, why did Jesus say, "Most assuredly, I say to you, he who believes in Me, the works that I do he will do also; and greater works than these he will do, because I go to My Father" (John 14:12)?

The question is, Whom are you going to believe?

BE YOUR SPIRITUAL SELF

There will be times when the Holy Spirit moves on you in ways that seem strange or abnormal to other people. However, the Spirit's activity is usually displayed in more usual ways as we go about our daily affairs—promptings to do this, to go there, to make a certain adjustment, or to contact a certain person. Sometimes we use the paradoxical phrase *naturally supernatural* to characterize such events.

Look, when you're operating in the Spirit and the supernatural, you have to get over any concerns about how weird you may look to the world. Pride is a surefire way to block the Spirit's flow. You're always going to rub against the grain of the natural realm if you're operating in the spiritual realm. At the same time, it's not necessary to develop super strange methodologies and practices in order to release the supernatural. Doing that is what gives Charismatics a bad name. Remember, it's not the manifestation that taps into the Spirit; it is the Spirit that produces the manifestation.

You can operate in the Spirit yet be yourself. All you have to do is let the Spirit flow through you according to your personality and gift mix. The Spirit knows what you need to do to release your faith. Operating in the Spirit is about how you, as a vessel filled with God, can release the power of His kingdom onto the scene. When you do, people will notice. Because people were being miraculously healed in the days of the twelve apostles, the locals "brought the sick out into the streets and laid them on beds and couches, that at least the shadow of Peter passing by might fall on some of them. Also a multitude gathered from the surrounding cities to Jerusalem, bringing sick people and those who were tormented by unclean spirits, and they were all healed" (Acts 5:15–16).

All were healed. Of course we understand that it is God who heals. But be careful not to adopt a mindset that says, "I am only a vessel of the Spirit. If I'm fortunate enough, He may use me. I don't really matter or have a part in what God is doing." That is not true humility; it is false humility, and it will rob you of your authority.

Jesus plainly said, "Heal the sick, cleanse the lepers, raise the dead, cast out demons. Freely you have received, freely give" (Matt. 10:8). He told His disciples to heal the sick. He didn't tell them to stop, pray, and check to see whether there was enough power in the Spirit to make it happen. Again, we know healing is the power of the Holy Spirit within us and the power of the Spirit upon the person for whom we pray. But Jesus gave us the authority to pray for a release of His power. It is a partnership. You are more than just a vessel. Adopt the mindset of carrying the miracle or being the miracle. Be the prophecy. Be the healer. Jesus the healer lives inside you. Own it.

Consider the examples of the apostles. They didn't walk up to sick people, hit the pause button before praying, and take them through the rigmarole of learning how to be humble and how to maintain a correct religious posture. They didn't try to qualify their actions. That's not what Jesus modeled to them, and it certainly wasn't what they modeled to other people. The apostles prayed for people.

Their prayers were short and hot, as Jesus' prayers had been. They simply said, "Be healed!"

Their prayers resulted not only in sicknesses being healed but also in calamities being averted. When Jesus was still with His disciples, "a great windstorm arose, and the waves beat into the boat, so that it was already filling. But He was in the stern, asleep on a pillow. And they awoke Him and said to Him, 'Teacher, do You not care that we are perishing?' Then He arose and rebuked the wind, and said to the sea, 'Peace, be still!' And the wind ceased and there was a great calm" (Mark 4:37–39).

Jesus' prayer in the boat was another short but effective prayer and another example of the spiritual realm influencing and altering the natural realm. We are really supernatural beings who live in physical bodies. We are equipped by the Holy Spirit to live and walk in the same miraculous power that Jesus does and His apostles did. This book will teach you how to do that.

Chapter 5

THE BELIEVER'S
MAKEUP

IN MANKIND GOD did something extraordinary. "God said, 'Let Us *make* man in Our image, according to Our likeness; let them have dominion'" (Gen. 1:26). After the initial creation of the cosmos and the earth with its plants and animals and all that went with it, God the Father, Son, and Holy Spirit—the *Us* in Genesis 1:26—did something different. Instead of creating just another living being, God the Trinity made man in His own image.

God formed Adam's body from the dust of the earth and then breathed spiritual life into him (Gen. 2:7). It was the kind of spiritual life that gave mankind dominion over the creation God made for them. Paul understood this when he wrote about believers having an outer man (a human body) and an inner man (a spiritual body). He explained that "even though our outward man is perishing, yet the inward man is being renewed day by day" (2 Cor. 4:16).

Paul then provided a deeper picture of our makeup, showing us to be made in three parts, rather than just two. He wrote, "Now may the God of peace Himself sanctify you completely; and may your whole spirit, soul, and body be preserved blameless at the coming of our Lord Jesus Christ" (1 Thess. 5:23). There is no contradiction in Paul's teachings on the outer man and inner man. Rather, he offered insight into what connects the two and allows them to function as one whole person.

Yes, we each have an outer man and an inner man, yet we each consist of three distinct parts. We understand ourselves better when we realize that each of us is a spirit and a soul living in a body. These are three areas of life in which we live and function. The following illustration helps us further visualize this reality.

The Believer's Makeup, Part 1

Inner Man and Outer Man
(2 Cor. 4:16; Eph. 3:16; Rom. 10:8–10)

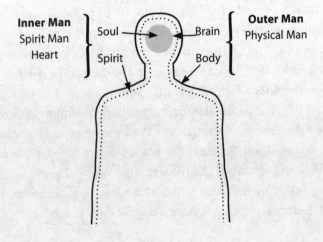

Inner Man
Spirit Man
Heart

Soul
Spirit

Brain
Body

Outer Man
Physical Man

The writer of Hebrews enlightens us to some additional spiritual truths about the spirit, soul, and body by saying the following: "The Word that God speaks is alive and full of power [making it active, operative, energizing, and effective]; it is sharper than any two-edged sword, penetrating to the dividing line of the breath of life (soul) and [the immortal] spirit, and of joints and marrow [of the deepest parts of our nature]" (4:12, AMPC).

First, notice that the Word of God is spiritually alive. It is the only thing that can define the difference between soul and spirit, and it shows us where their connecting line is. Second, the soul can be distinguished from the spirit but not separated from it. Most of us know that the inner man is separated from the outer man when a believer dies and goes to heaven. In heaven, though, the believer retains all the soul's faculties that are attributed to the mind, such as personality, reasoning, and emotions. Third, the Word of God discerns the physical nature. This is what Paul meant by "joints and marrow." Our Creator knows every part of our existence, and the Holy Spirit reveals it to us in His Word. The next illustration shows how Hebrews 4:12 and 1 Thessalonians 5:23 flow together.

The Believer's Makeup, Part 2

Spirit, Soul, and Body
(1 Thess. 5:23; Heb. 4:12)

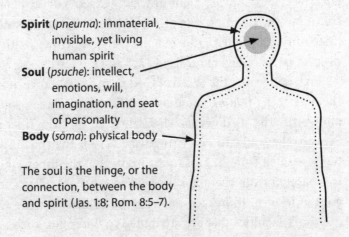

Spirit (*pneuma*): immaterial, invisible, yet living human spirit

Soul (*psuche*): intellect, emotions, will, imagination, and seat of personality

Body (*sōma*): physical body

The soul is the hinge, or the connection, between the body and spirit (Jas. 1:8; Rom. 8:5–7).

Concerning the key words *spirit*, *soul*, and *body* mentioned in 1 Thessalonians 5:23, biblical commentator Gary H. Everett noted,

> The process of sanctification begins in the spirit and proceeds through the soul and into the body. This verse lists the three-fold make-up of man in this order of sanctification: spirit, soul, and body. God initially gives the born-again believer a new, recreated spirit in his inner man. The believer then begins to sanctify his mind through an understanding of the Word of God. This allows the believer to conduct his actions and lifestyle in a manner that conducts him along a journey of peace in every area of his life. Many believers have been born again, but they have not renewed their minds with the

Word of God. Therefore, they incur many unnecessary problems in life because of this deficiency in their minds and bodies. The Spirit of God has been poured forth into the life of every believer to guide him into a journey of peace in every aspect of his make-up: spirit, soul, and body....The spirit is the heart of man; the soul is man's mind, emotions, and intellect; and the body is man's physical body.[1]

Adequately defining the spirit, soul, and body is foundational in strengthening our abilities to walk in the Spirit. These truths are the nuts and bolts of our makeup and cannot be overemphasized. The Greek term rendered "spirit" in 1 Thessalonians 5:23 is *pneuma*, which refers to the immaterial, invisible human spirit.[2] In English when we speak of pneumatic equipment, we're indicating air-driven devices such as jackhammers or air compressors. You can't see the air, but it is present and has force. Likewise, our spirits are invisible and eternal. They are the higher spiritual parts of us that have life and function in the spiritual realm.

In the same verse the Greek word translated "soul" is *psuche*.[3] This is the part of our inner man—namely, the intellect, emotions, will, imagination, and personality—that animates the body.[4] The English words *psyche* and *psychology* come from this word. In the New Testament the term *soul* (*psuche*) can be understood as encompassing the mind, though it isn't limited to that. It also refers to natural or rational life,[5] integrating all the mental processes. The soul is what enables you to function in the rational aspects of life. The soul can also be considered a person's inner consciousness. It differentiates one person from everybody else as much as, or perhaps more than, the body does. This differentiation ensures that no two people are the same.

The word translated "body" is the Greek term *sōma*, which refers to the physical body or frame.[6] You've probably heard of somatic illness, which relates to the physical body. Our bodies function on this earth and give us life. As I previously mentioned, we can think of our bodies as our earth suits; they allow the spirit man to access physical creation. If the earth suit stops working, we can't stay here any longer.

Paul reminds us that "to be absent from the body [is] to be present with the Lord" (2 Cor. 5:8). Thank God for His divine plan to reunite us with our glorified bodies at the resurrection. Eternity is waiting for the believer's complete redemption. Paul wanted believers to be assured that the Lord had such a plan when he wrote, "May your whole spirit, soul, and body be preserved blameless at the coming of our Lord Jesus Christ" (1 Thess. 5:23).

Vine's Expository Dictionary of New Testament Words explains that "the word [*sōma*] is also used for physical nature, as distinct from *pneuma*, 'the spiritual nature,' e.g., 1Cr 5:3, and from *psuche*, 'the soul,' e.g., 1Th 5:23."[7] An important principle to point out is that the soul is the hinge between the spirit and the body. Paul said that "the mind set on the flesh is death, but the mind set on the Spirit is life and peace" (Rom. 8:6, NASB). The soul can mentally process both physical and spiritual information. But the illumination of God's Spirit is what quickens our understanding of spiritual information.

Picture this: When you enter a room, you typically walk through a door that is attached to its frame by hinges. The door could not function without being connected to the wall in this way. A hinge that is connected to both the wall (frame) and the door allows them to work as one unit. Similarly, the soul allows the human spirit and body to function together. This isn't a perfect analogy, but it shows us the soul's capabilities in both the spiritual realm and the physical realm.

James alluded to this when he talked about a double-minded man who chooses to yield to worldly pressures instead of the Holy Spirit's leading. "[For being as he is] a man of two minds (hesitating, dubious, irresolute), [he is] unstable and unreliable and uncertain about everything [he thinks, feels, decides]" (Jas. 1:8, AMPC). Young's Literal Translation puts this verse a little differently, saying, "A two-souled man [is] unstable in all his ways."

The soul's ability to process information from both realms is not the problem James was addressing; his concern was our tendency to meditate on fleshly matters while ignoring the Spirit. However, to be spiritually minded or carnally minded is our choice, and what we choose determines whether we are operating in faith or doubt. But notice this critical key to unlocking the supernatural: The voice of God and the gifts of the Holy Spirit rise from within and flow through the spirit of your mind, which brings us to our next illustration.

The Believer's Makeup, Part 3

God's Seed Within
(1 John 3:9; Prov. 4:23)

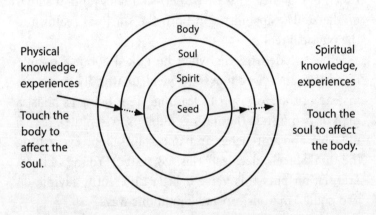

Physical knowledge, experiences

Touch the body to affect the soul.

Body
Soul
Spirit
Seed

Spiritual knowledge, experiences

Touch the soul to affect the body.

This illustration highlights simply the progressive flow of both spiritual and physical knowledge within us. It serves to complement the concepts of body, soul, and spirit presented in part 2. Notice that the spirit is at the center. The soul is next, and the body is on the outside. Note also that all worldly, physical knowledge comes from the outside through the body and to the soul. In contrast, all spiritual knowledge (everything from God's Word and Spirit) originates in our spirits and then flows out through the soul to affect the body.

When you call out to Jesus and ask Him to save you, you receive the God seed (which I like to call the Christ seed) into your heart. As 1 John 3:9 says, "Whoever has been born of God does not sin, for His seed remains in him." Your spirit is regenerated, born again, and changed into the image of God's dear Son. You become a new creation in Christ Jesus. Nothing that happens to you on the outside can forcibly remove the Christ seed from your spirit. Everything that the devil and the world's circumstances bring against you comes from the outside. Those things touch the body to affect the soul, but they cannot penetrate your spirit.

This is so important because most people are trained to live from the outside to the inside. Their focuses, and therefore their self-awarenesses, purely depend on what happens to them. When they hear doctrines of works and legalism, they think that whatever happens externally can change and alter the human spirit.

It does not. You can sin in your flesh, yet your spirit remains a new creation in Christ Jesus. People are victimized in many ways in the outside world, and this causes changes in their bodies and their minds. But it does not penetrate, affect, hurt, dampen, or lessen the spirit that is within them.

Why is this significant? Because the enemy uses sin that is done to us (victimization) and sin that is done by us (personal failures) to attack us with condemnation and consciousness of sin (Heb. 10:2, 22). Satan will try to convince us that our human spirits have been damaged and therefore we are corrupted, rejected by God, and disqualified from walking in the Spirit.

Your value is founded on what the heavenly Father deemed your worth to be—the blood sacrifice of Jesus, "the Lamb slain from the foundation of the world" (Rev. 13:8). In Christ Jesus your spirit is regenerated. And from the Holy Spirit, who lives within your human spirit, come healing and redemptive power. Regardless of what has happened to you or what you have done, the Holy Spirit and the Word of God within you can alter the effects of those events. The Spirit and the Word don't undo what has happened or erase responsibility for your actions, but they can miraculously disempower the effects of past circumstances by healing damage and bringing restoration. This is a redemptive act, and it is very good news!

Look at the first illustration again. You'll see that your spirit fits within your body and that your soul is linked to your brain, your onboard computer that handles the physical information and stimuli in your life. Your brain is a wonderful, intricate organ created by God to do amazing things on many levels. The average brain weighs only three or so pounds, but it contains about eighty-six billion neurons, or brain cells. Each cell is connected to other cells, totaling as much as one quadrillion connections.[8] Award-winning physicist Michio Kaku noted that the brain "is the most complicated object in the known universe."[9] When we finally discover its true potential, I think we'll be astounded.

We sometimes hear people talking about soulish believers, which is usually meant as a reference to believers who are carnally minded, given to the lusts and reasonings of the flesh. Assuming that accusation is true, we ought not to disparage the human soul. The soul is part of who we are. To grow in the Lord's nurturing and admonition, we yield our souls to the Holy Spirit. But "the good fight of faith" (1 Tim. 6:12) starts in the mind. It is the battlefield where the war is primarily waged. Since the soul is the hinge between the spirit and body, and because it accesses knowledge from both the spiritual realm and the natural realm, the mind is where we decide what information we will believe and follow.

Paul explained that "the weapons of our warfare are not carnal but mighty in God for pulling down strongholds, casting down arguments and every high thing that exalts itself against the knowledge of God, bringing every thought into captivity to the obedience of Christ" (2 Cor. 10:4–5). The mind is the battleground where the decision to walk in the Spirit or to walk in the flesh is made. When we yield to the Word and the Spirit, our faith grows and we operate in the supernatural. "*Now faith* is the assurance (the confirmation, the title deed) of the things [we] hope for, being the proof of things [we] do not see and the conviction of their reality [faith perceiving as real fact what is not revealed to the senses]" (Heb. 11:1, AMPC).

To effectively walk in the Spirit, we need to be aware of our perceptions in relation to the spirit, soul, and body. *Perception* is the ability to receive, identify, and interpret sensory information.[10] It involves an awareness of an environment. God created us with physical and spiritual senses that allow us to perceive the physical and spiritual realms, as our next illustration shows.

The Believer's Makeup, Part 4

Perceptions: Spirit, Soul, and Body
(1 Thess. 5:23; Heb. 4:12)

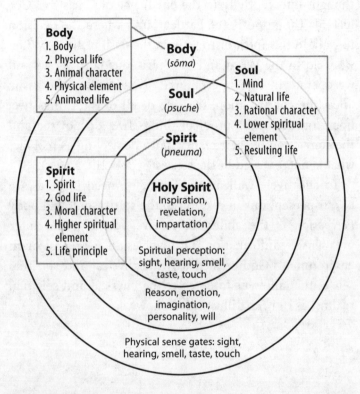

Body
1. Body
2. Physical life
3. Animal character
4. Physical element
5. Animated life

Body
(*sōma*)

Soul
1. Mind
2. Natural life
3. Rational character
4. Lower spiritual element
5. Resulting life

Soul
(*psuche*)

Spirit
(*pneuma*)

Spirit
1. Spirit
2. God life
3. Moral character
4. Higher spiritual element
5. Life principle

Holy Spirit
Inspiration, revelation, impartation

Spiritual perception: sight, hearing, smell, taste, touch

Reason, emotion, imagination, personality, will

Physical sense gates: sight, hearing, smell, taste, touch

Because we are new creations in Christ Jesus, the Holy Spirit resides in our spirits. From the inside He provides inspirations, revelations, and impartations that are communicated through a variety of means. We can receive impressions, prompts, hunches, or senses of knowing—none of which can be explained by natural means. You may hear what the Bible calls "a still small voice" deep within your consciousness (1 Kings 19:12). Or we can see images form within us that visually transmit the Spirit's will to us. That's what I call inside information.

God's Spirit is an ever-present source of revelation that leads and inspires us. However, information is not the only thing the Spirit supplies. There is also power—redeeming power, maturing power, ministry power, and warfare power. Everything we need that pertains to life and godliness is in the Holy Spirit's indwelling presence. (See 2 Peter 1:3.) Our human spirits possess spiritual senses of perception—sight, hearing, smell, taste, and touch. The Holy Spirit uses these spiritual senses to communicate with our spirits and then to channel information to the spirits of our minds.

That is why God made us with spiritual senses. How else could we live in the spiritual realm? "He who has ears to hear, let him hear!" said Jesus in Matthew 11:15. Isaiah declared, "In the year that King Uzziah died, I saw the Lord sitting on a throne" (Isa. 6:1). King David wrote, "Oh, taste and see that the LORD is good" (Ps. 34:8). These are more than figurative sayings; they point to a very real spiritual realm in which we can see God, hear Him, and feel His presence.

Yet we also live in a physical realm, where our bodies have physical senses of perception—sight, hearing, smell, taste, and touch. Because this realm is familiar to us, it doesn't need much explanation. I must point out, however, that our physical senses (which are connected to the human nervous system) channel information to the rational parts of our minds. The Holy Spirit impresses His information on the spirits of our minds (Eph. 4:23). The spirit of the mind and the rational mind are both within the soul. It's there that reason, emotion, imagination, personality, and will are influenced by the spiritual and physical realms. The more we yield to the Spirit, the more spiritually mature we become and the more we discover His ways.

God's Word is a major part of this process. His Word is God breathed and full of His life and power, which are released into our souls by revelation from the Holy Spirit, transforming our minds and supervising our bodies. I've previously touched on this idea in relation to Paul's letter to the Romans, in which Paul told believers, "Present your bodies a living sacrifice, holy, acceptable to God, which is your reasonable service. And do not be conformed to this world, but be transformed by the renewing of your mind" (Rom. 12:1–2).

COMPARING SPIRIT, SOUL, AND BODY

As I wrap up this chapter's explanation of the human makeup, here are a few notes and a chart comparing the spirit, soul, and body of the born-again believer.

Spirit	Soul	Body
1. Spirit	1. Mind	1. Body
2. God life	2. Natural life	2. Physical life
3. Moral character	3. Rational character	3. Animal character
4. Higher spiritual element	4. Lower spiritual element	4. Physical element
5. Life principle	5. Resulting life	5. Animated life

- The spirit has God life. The soul has natural life. The body has physical life.

- The spirit has moral character. The soul has rational character. The body has animal character.

- The spirit has a higher spiritual element. The soul has a lower spiritual element. The body has a physical element.

- The spirit has the life principle. The soul has resulting life. The body has animated life.

Here are some questions you need to ask yourself: Do I want to walk in the Spirit and navigate heavenly places? Do I want to have dreams and visions, hear the voice of God, and learn the communication system of heaven? Do I want to pray for the healing of the sick and the binding of demonic spirits? Do I want to do all the works Jesus did and also the greater works He mentioned in John 14:12?

If the answer is yes, then you need to operate from the spirit, or inner man, under the power of God's Word and Spirit. That requires learning how to "be renewed in the spirit of [your] mind" (Eph. 4:23). As Paul told the Colossians, we need to "put on the new man who is renewed in knowledge according to the image of Him who created him" (Col. 3:10). No one will do this perfectly, but we can become more skilled at it as we follow Christ.

Over the course of my Christian life I've learned much about how to see, hear, and feel things in the spiritual realm, and there is always more to learn. I exhort you to become aware that the real you—your spirit and soul—are on the inside. Then believe that you can learn to be more conscious of your spiritual senses. You did it when you received Jesus. The Holy Spirit quickened your heart to your need to accept the Savior, and you acted on it. You didn't do that apart from what I have just shared with you.

That means you can continue walking in the Spirit for the rest of your life.

Bear in mind that to remain healthy, strong, and productive in your body, you have to establish proper diet, exercise, and rest regimens. Your mind processes vast amounts of knowledge, and you exercise your mind through thinking and reasoning. Your inner man requires a healthy diet of God's Word and inspiration from His Spirit. Then you need to use faith and prayer to keep your inner man exercised, sharp, and strong. As a side note, praying in your spiritual prayer language (tongues) is a supercharged way to do this!

When a believer grows in his or her ability to walk in the Spirit, something remarkable happens—the outer man becomes trained to discern the difference between good and evil and then choose what is good. This truth is brought out in the Book of Hebrews.

> For though by this time you ought to be teachers, you need someone to teach you again the first principles of the oracles of God; and you have come to need milk and not solid food. For everyone who partakes only of milk is unskilled in the word of righteousness, for he is a babe. But solid food belongs to those who are of full age, that is, those who by reason of use have their senses exercised to discern both good and evil.
>
> —HEBREWS 5:12–14

Let me close this chapter with one last point: God created humanity to live and function in proper order. That means the regenerated human spirit rules over the soul, which directs the physical body. Through the fall of Adam and Eve the divine order was disrupted. Humanity was separated from God by spiritual death, and the cravings, desires, and emotions of the flesh began to rule.

Through Jesus and the new creation, God has restored proper order. Walking in the Spirit brings the regenerated human spirit back into ascendancy over the soul, so the soul can again direct the physical body. Interestingly, this proper order puts us right where God wants us to be, in grace, faith, love, and righteousness. And when we are aligned with our Creator—spirit, soul, and body—we become more effective warriors in the Lion's army.

Chapter 6

QUALIFIED TO WALK IN THE SPIRIT

A FTER RECOGNIZING HOW God has wonderfully made us in three parts (spirit, soul, and body), we need to also understand that receiving Jesus as our Savior means we are qualified to walk in the Spirit. The truth is that through Jesus, God not only qualifies us but *expects* us to walk in the Spirit.

There is nothing more satisfying than the truly Spirit-filled life, which is rich with hearing God's voice and experiencing supernatural manifestations of His Spirit. If we are new creations and are indwelled by the Holy Spirit, whom God put within us, why *wouldn't* we walk in the Spirit? Isn't that what He created us to do?

The answer is a resounding *yes*!

Yet so many believers skip this critical part, settling for religious rules and rituals rather than authentically connecting with the Holy Spirit, experiencing His presence, and receiving His step-by-step guidance—even though walking in the Spirit is part of our divine calling as born-again children of God.

Paul encouraged those in the church to walk out their identities as new creations indwelled by the Holy Spirit and saved by grace. That's why he wrote in Galatians 5:25, "If we live in the Spirit, let us also walk in the Spirit." Another translation says, "Let us keep in step with the Spirit" (NIV). Whatever the translation the implication could not be clearer: It is possible to "live in the Spirit" (being saved) yet not "walk in the Spirit."

Unfortunately, that is exactly where most believers live. It is not a loss only for them, because the calling to walk in the Spirit is not only for their sakes. Walking in the Spirit allows born-again people to be conduits through which the Spirit can flow and touch others. Walking in the Spirit is also a must if we are to be effective warriors in the Lion's army. We need to have keen spiritual ears attuned to our leader's every order so we are ready to engage at a moment's notice.

Fortunately, the Lord doesn't call us and then leave us unprepared. After He qualifies and expects us to walk in the Spirit, He gives us principles to learn and actions to take. These enhance how well we walk, but we must cooperate. Not only can we learn to live a truly Spirit-filled life, but we must want it and pursue it. Hebrews 11:6 declares, "He is a rewarder of those who diligently seek Him."

The things of the Spirit are part of our reward. In the next chapter we will explore spiritual gifts and how they relate to walking in the Spirit, as well as how your spiritual gifts can be used to minister to the people around you.

For now, however, let's consider some foundational principles that will help us walk in the Spirit.

APPROVAL, AUTHORITY, AND ANOINTING

Like humans who are made with three parts (spirit, soul, and body), God consists of three persons in one. I say *consists of* because God, unlike humans, was not made. He is eternal, meaning He always was, and He exists outside time. Unlike humans, God is not one being divided into three parts. Rather, He is one being consisting of three distinct, whole, and absolute persons—God the Father, God the Son, and God the Holy Spirit. They are three personalities, yet they are one.

This is what we call the Trinity. Each person of the Godhead is equal and fully connected to the others while having distinct roles. This is a difficult concept for our limited minds to comprehend, but it's a foundational, biblical truth that is critical to living a Spirit-filled life. It's important because each person of the Trinity influences and empowers us in a specific way. Let's look at some of those ways.

1. God the Father gives us approval.

Father God bestows His blessing on all His children, along with the right to be who He created them to be. Not only does He bless us, but He loves us, as Scripture shows.

> Most assuredly, I say to you, whatever you ask the Father in My name He will give you....for the Father Himself loves you.
>
> —JOHN 16:23, 27

> Blessed be the God and Father of our Lord Jesus
> Christ, who has blessed us with every spiritual
> blessing in the heavenly places in Christ.
>
> —EPHESIANS 1:3

God the Father has openly declared His *approval* to His children. We have every right to be alive and blessed by Him. Because we are accepted through the beloved Lord Jesus, there is no such thing as a child of God who is unqualified to walk in the Spirit or conduct spiritual affairs. In Christ we are unconditionally loved, accepted, valued, and approved by the Father.

> Blessed be the God and Father of our Lord Jesus
> Christ...just as He chose us in Him before the
> foundation of the world, that we should be holy
> and without blame before Him in love, having pre-
> destined us to adoption as sons by Jesus Christ to
> Himself, according to the good pleasure of His will,
> to the praise of the glory of His grace, by which He
> made us accepted in the Beloved.
>
> —EPHESIANS 1:3–6

The approval I'm referring to here relates directly to the new birth and to who you *are* in the Spirit rather than what you *do* because of Him. Of course, the Father wants to approve of the attitudes and behaviors you display under the pressure of trials. As His child, you are mandated to grow through the sanctification process, proving yourself to be mature and steadfast, resisting sin's temptations, and staying spiritually strong during life's tribulations.

It's been said that Christians are like unmarked tea bags.

You don't know what they are made of until you put them in hot water. James affirmed this notion when he wrote, "Blessed is the man who endures temptation; for when he has been *approved*, he will receive the crown of life which the Lord has promised to those who love Him" (Jas. 1:12).

From a natural standpoint people need approval from their parents. Parental love and approval help build strong, confident character in children. This approval becomes an anchor in children's unstable worlds and adds meaning to their existences. Many adults struggle in life because they are trying to fill the approval receptors that weren't filled by their parents when they were growing up. I'm grateful to God for giving me wonderful, loving parents; I've met scores of people who didn't have that blessing.

In the Spirit it's the same way. We need our heavenly Father's approval. This parallel is not exact, however, because God is always a good Father. How, then, do we know that we have His approval? We believe what He says *to* us and *about* us in His Word. Unfortunately, what He says can become distorted. Carnal reasoning or incorrect Bible teaching can convince some believers that the Father is withholding His approval from them. Devilish condemnation tells them that they made mistakes in life because they *are* mistakes.

This attack against their inner beings suggests that the Father somehow messed up by leaving something out of the new-creation recipe or by not using enough of His power to perfect the job. But it's time for us to realize that God doesn't make mistakes. Traumas and missteps happen in life, but they cannot damage the Christ seed inside us.

One of the common errors believers can make is called transference. Subconsciously, the believer transfers an earthly parent's face onto God the Father, in effect remaking God in the parent's image. If you were fortunate enough to have loving, nourishing parents, as I was, this is usually not a big issue, although all parents fall short at times. But if your parents were abusive, emotionally distant, or addicted, or if they had other dysfunctional behaviors that caused you pain, transference can become a major obstacle by distorting your perception of God. The enemy can turn this false belief into a stronghold that keeps you from drawing close to the Father.

This is opposite to what the truth does. God is always a good Father. He loves His children, and He made each of us in His own image. He approves of His image in us, and so should we. He has already put His stamp of approval on our lives. Yes, He corrects us. But there is a difference between the enemy's condemnation and how the Father convicts us of wrong attitudes or behaviors when we mess up.

The false accuser says, "You messed up again. Look at what a dirtbag you are. Because God is so disappointed, He could never love you. You can't keep going back to Him. He's tired of you." Those thoughts are lies straight from the accuser. The Father never treats His kids that way. He never tires of us coming home. His forgiveness is unlimited and supernatural. The inner voice and feelings that come from the Father tell us that our mistakes are real but not consistent with who we are as His children. He then shows us how to address our missteps through repentance, without attacking the work He has done within us. "For [He is] good, and ready to forgive, and abundant in mercy to all those who call upon [Him]" (Ps. 86:5).

If you are His, you are approved.

2. Jesus, God the Son, gives us authority.

The Lord Jesus grants and delegates to all believers the *permission* to use His name, giving them the *right to act* on His behalf.

> And Jesus came and spoke to them, saying, "All authority has been given to Me in heaven and on earth. Go therefore and make disciples of all the nations, baptizing them in the name of the Father and of the Son and of the Holy Spirit."
>
> —MATTHEW 28:18–19

> Behold, I give you the authority to trample on serpents and scorpions, and over all the power of the enemy, and nothing shall by any means hurt you.
>
> —LUKE 10:19

> If you ask anything in My name, I will do it.
>
> —JOHN 14:14

Approval from the Father is the *right to be*. Delegated authority from Jesus is the *right to act*. The Lord Jesus grants all believers permission to walk in the Spirit with authority. Where does this spiritual authority come from? It comes from Jesus! Where did He get it? On the cross. There He defeated Satan for us; then He rose from the dead for us and gave us His authority.

When God created the human race, He endowed it with spiritual and physical dominion on the earth. Then through Adam and Eve's fall Satan was able to usurp their spiritual authority and use it against them and their descendants. When Satan tempted Jesus in the wilderness by showing Him the kingdoms of the earth, he boasted, "All this authority I will give You, and their glory; for this has been delivered to me, and I give it to whomever I wish" (Luke 4:6). Satan stole that *authority* from Adam and Eve and thus became the god of this world—but that's *god* with a small *g*. The great I Am, the one eternal God with a capital *G*, is outside time and already had a plan in motion to take back what Satan stole. But He had to do it legally.

Jesus didn't refute what Satan said in the wilderness; He refused to be tricked into worshipping the deceiver. (See Luke 4:1–15.) Jesus understood God's plan of salvation and chose to die on the cross and rise again. Through His obedience He broke Satan's power off all who would receive Him and His saving grace. Through salvation, spiritual authority was restored to believers. "Therefore submit to God. Resist the devil and he will flee from you" (Jas. 4:7).

It's important to realize, however, that spiritual authority covers much more than resisting the devil. Jesus taught His evangelistic team that His church would be able to bind the unlawful works of Satan on earth while at the same time loosing Jesus' lawful works in their place. (See Matthew 16:19.) Jesus cast demons out of people, yet He also healed the sick, raised the dead, walked on water, calmed storms, multiplied food, and set hearts free. Jesus used His authority in all areas and then told us, "He who believes in Me, the works that I do he will do also; and greater works than these he will do, because I go to My Father" (John 14:12).

Our Lord and Savior is known by one name expressed with different spellings in innumerable languages—Yeshua (Hebrew), Iēsous (Greek), Jesús (Spanish), Gesù (Italian), and so on. Jesus answers to every one of those spellings and pronunciations because they all are Him. Satan and his demons are paralyzed, cast out, and defeated by Jesus' name, because it releases the authority He delegated to us. In whatever language it's spoken, the precious name of Jesus represents His entire character, as well as His position and power. To say His name in faith is to call upon who He is in all His glory. He gave His name to us for that very purpose. Mark's Gospel says it this way: "Everyone who believes me will be able to do wonderful things. By using my name they will force out demons, and they will speak new languages. They will handle snakes and will drink poison and not be hurt. They will also heal sick people by placing their hands on them" (Mark 16:17–18, CEV).

We are entitled to walk in the Spirit authoritatively; Jesus gave us the right to act on His behalf.

3. God the Holy Spirit gives us the anointing.

The Holy Spirit offers every Christian *the anointing*, which is spiritual power, or the ability to act with His supernatural help. The Scriptures speak openly of this power, which Jesus exemplified.

> God anointed Jesus of Nazareth with the Holy Spirit and with power, who went about doing good and healing all who were oppressed by the devil, for God was with Him.
>
> —ACTS 10:38

> But you shall receive power when the Holy Spirit has come upon you.
>
> —ACTS 1:8

> But the anointing which you have received from
> Him abides in you, and you do not need that anyone
> teach you; but as the same anointing teaches you
> concerning all things, and is true, and is not a lie,
> and just as it has taught you, you will abide in Him.
>
> —1 JOHN 2:27

Approval from the Father is the *right to be*, and delegated authority from Jesus is the *right to act*. Now, we learn that anointing from the Holy Spirit is the *ability* to act. This means the Spirit provides us with the spiritual wisdom and power necessary to live a supernatural existence. No wonder Jesus called the Holy Spirit "the Helper" (John 14:26). He helps us be who the Father created us to be and do what Jesus has called us to do. God qualifies, Jesus authorizes, and the Holy Spirit empowers.

So what is anointing? There are several Greek words for *anointing* used in the New Testament. The following is a basic summary of their meanings as they relate to our lives. The word *anointing* means the pouring on of oil or the rubbing in of ointment. Physically, it's similar to applying lotion to your dry hands to soften them again. Spiritually, though, anointing symbolizes the refreshment and empowerment provided by God's Spirit as special endowments (or as supernatural enabling). Through the anointing the Holy Spirit also consecrates us, or sets us apart, for specific positions and functions within the body of Christ.

Sometimes the anointing manifests as spiritual electricity—the spiritual energy that powers everything in the kingdom of heaven. At least that energy is a major part of it. The anointing is also associated with the Holy Spirit's divine presence, meaning that you'll find anointing wherever the Spirit is moving and in whatever the Spirit is involved in.

Felt awareness of the Spirit's presence is difficult to describe. We can feel it individually or in groups. However, we witness the effects of His presence in various ways. We may feel a compelling urgency to tell someone about Jesus and then experience special boldness to do it. When we lay hands on someone who is sick and pray for them, we may feel tingling or heat in our hands and then see the person miraculously healed.

The anointing is power, and we can experience the presence of that power in tangible ways. In gatherings, for example, believers are often moved to weep, laugh, or enter into a holy silence without the help of any natural stimulus. Some people may shake uncontrollably or fall on the floor. Others can become animated with joy or abundance of energy. Wherever God's glory is, it will be accompanied by spiritual anointing.

In my experience and ministry the anointing seems to manifest in different ways according to what the Holy Spirit wants to accomplish. There are distinct anointings for distinct purposes. I've learned over time how to tell what the Spirit is doing by the anointing that is present. Worship, teaching, salvation, healing, and prophecy each carry a different anointing. I've found the same to be true of each Charismatic gift of the Spirit that's in operation.

We can expect the Holy Spirit's anointing to be within us and upon us for everything we're called to do. In the Word we see indications that the anointings within us empower us to walk in the Spirit and supernaturally deal with external circumstances. Learning to be sensitive to the anointing is key if we are to work with it and not against it.

THREE MEASURES

Before we discuss the key measures of ministry, grace, and faith, let's take a more general look at the ways in which God equips believers for life and ministry. For believers there is what I call the baselevel of our inheritance in Jesus. I'm referring to God's grace and provision being equal for all His children. We all have the fullness of Christ, and every believer is qualified for every spiritual blessing in Him. This was a major emphasis of the previous section on approval, authority, and anointing. Each of us can learn the ways of the Spirit.

There are also personal add-ons, as I call them. I use this term because they are personalized by God to fit our spiritual callings and assignments. The Spirit fine-tunes them to match our personalities, natural talents, spiritual gift mixes, and specialized anointings. They are not above the baselevel of our inheritance but are more highly focused and directed aspects of it, producing unique applications that equip and empower believers for their specific lives and ministries.

It's amazing how the Holy Spirit weaves together millions of individual threads to create the tapestry known as the body of Christ. The threads are all made of the same spiritual material, but each adds something unique. The tapestry is alive, moving, and changing but always presenting the image of Jesus. The more we understand our parts, the greater fulfillment and impacts we experience and the less disappointments and grief the enemy can throw at us.

Now, let's look at what the Word describes as measures and how three measures provide structure to your unique ministry. The word *measure* denotes a set portion. You can think of measures as boundaries for your ministry. So no one misunderstands, there are no measures on your salvation or Spirit baptism. Boundaries for ministry simply define where and how you will have your greatest influence for Jesus. They mark off the areas in which you will discover increased manifestations of the supernatural.

1. The measure of ministry

The measure of ministry involves the sphere of influence to which God has called you. The apostle Paul addressed this matter in his second letter to the church at Corinth.

> For we dare not class ourselves or compare ourselves with those who commend themselves. But they, measuring themselves by themselves, and comparing themselves among themselves, are not wise. We, however, will not boast beyond measure, but within the limits of the sphere which God appointed us—a sphere which especially includes you. For we are not overextending ourselves (as though our authority did not extend to you), for it was to you that we came with the gospel of Christ; not boasting of things beyond measure, that is, in other men's labors, but having hope, that as your faith is increased, we shall be greatly enlarged by you in our sphere, to preach the gospel in the regions beyond you, and not to boast in another man's sphere of accomplishment.
>
> —2 CORINTHIANS 10:12–16

The limits of the sphere of your God-given ministry are your ministry's platform. It is a spiritual platform that has a spiritual size, shape, and theme. It's hard to define spiritual matters sometimes, but the platform's dimensions are made of things such as spiritual gifts, callings, and anointings. Groups of people are also involved.

Collectively, these dimensions create a sphere of influence. We are always most effective within our own spheres of influence. For example, speaking of himself, Paul said, "I was appointed a preacher, an apostle, and a teacher of the Gentiles" (2 Tim. 1:11). The Scriptures seem to indicate that Paul was willing to minister to anyone about Jesus. But it is apparent that his main ministry was to the Gentiles, and it was in that ministry that he had his greatest influence.

From my experience our ministry platform has grown and changed in many ways over the years. I have also learned that trying to take on someone else's ministry (or any ministry to which I'm not called) is frustrating. Likewise, trying to do my God-ordained ministry by other people's methods is ineffective. I can learn principles from other people, but I cannot model myself after them.

When CK and I were first Spirit-filled, we were so on fire for God that we would talk to anyone about Jesus. Moving in the gifts of the Spirit, we went looking for people to whom we could minister and for whom we could pray with hope for miracles. So many people were saved, baptized in the Spirit, and miraculously healed that we knew God was with us. Our passion never diminished, but we began to notice patterns in our effectiveness. Sometimes we were more effective than other times. In certain settings the anointing was stronger, and the gifts operated more fluently.

As we became more skilled in spiritual things, we learned to listen to the voice of the Holy Spirit and to work with the patterns that developed. We realized that both those things were connected with our measures of ministry. Also, we identified each other's giftings and anointings and began deferring to whomever had the stronger anointing for the situation that arose.

CK and I entered full-time ministry and were ordained into an evangelistic association. We traveled to many cities, preaching the Word with signs following. A little over a year later, the Lord led us into pastoral ministry and then eventually into ministry as prophets. Forty-six years and four cities later, we are in Las Vegas ministering in a studio, with a local congregation and a worldwide, online congregation. Our platform of ministry and influence has grown and morphed into what it is today. We have done our best to be true to God's calling every step of the way, even when some of our closest friends and family members didn't understand our steps or tried to stop us.

Remember, if you are "faithful over a few things," God "will make you ruler over many things" (Matt. 25:23). God will bless what you have, and He will enlarge your platform of influence as you go. Staying on your own platform of ministry brings fulfillment and impact, but getting off your platform or onto someone else's brings grief. You cannot be a jack-of-all-trades, because that would make you a master of nothing. You have to focus on what the Holy Spirit is leading you to do.

2. The measure of grace

Grace is the *atmosphere* of God's favor, which empowers you within your sphere. Paul spoke of how God measures His grace to us.

> I, therefore, the prisoner of the Lord, beseech you to walk worthy of the calling with which you were called....[knowing that] to each one of us *grace* was given according to the *measure* of Christ's gift.
>
> —EPHESIANS 4:1, 7

Your measure of grace is the same size as your platform of ministry. It is not smaller than your ministry platform, and it does not extend beyond it. God gives you the grace you need to fulfill your ministry. Therefore, His favor and empowerment to you are perfectly measured to match your platform. This is not the saving grace that extends to all; it is a ministry grace for specifically called believers.

Grace is generally defined as unmerited favor. However, there is also a contextual definition of how the word is used in relation to certain scriptures. Often in God's Word, *grace* is used to define God's favor toward what we do. It is not about earning His favor to qualify for ministry but about functioning within the specific favor He places over the ministry. This idea also applies to spiritual gifts and works of faith.

Here's the working definition of *grace* that I use in my teachings: *Grace* is the unmerited favor of God that enables me to be who He created me to be and to do what He has called me to do.

Earlier, I mentioned CK and our ministry journey together. Every change in ministry required a change in grace. When the platform altered, the Holy Spirit breathed onto it the grace that we needed to take ownership of that platform of ministry. Many times over the years, I've been asked to do things that were in direct opposition to (1) what the Lord called me to do, or (2) how He called me to do it. I've had to respond by saying, "That's not my grace." I've said it that way in part because if I said, "It's not my ministry or my calling," some people might have assumed that I was making excuses for something I didn't want to do. No— if I get out of my grace, it will lead to some kind of grief.

3. The measure of faith

Faith is the *confident trust* in God that motivates you within your sphere and your grace. Paul mentioned the measure of faith in very personal terms.

> For I say, through the grace given to me, to everyone who is among you, not to think of himself more highly than he ought to think, but to think soberly, as God has dealt to each one a *measure of faith*.... as we have many members in one body, but all the members do not have the same function.
>
> —ROMANS 12:3–4

Your measure of faith is the same size as your measure of grace. Remember, this is not a reference to the baselevel faith of all believers. This is faith for ministry. For example, I have the faith to be a prophet who lives in Las Vegas and is writing a book about the Lion's army. I daresay that you don't have this specific faith because it involves my grace and not yours. By the same token, however, I'll never have the faith to do what you are called to do.

A basic principle to remember is that you can have faith only for what has been promised in grace. Another way to say this is that spiritual faith is a response to God's grace. Faith is so vitally important for two reasons:

1. Faith is our part and our responsibility. The Holy Spirit can initiate wonderful things in our lives, but if we don't believe Him and act on them, nothing will happen.

2. Faith activates the Spirit's power, which is incorporated into grace. This principle is one of the ways of the Spirit.

Now that we have laid these foundational principles for walking in the Spirit, we are ready to move on toward a fuller understanding of various spiritual gifts and how we can apply them as we walk with Christ.

Chapter 7

SPIRITUAL GIFTS, PART 1

I N 2010 I was caught up to heaven's throne room by the Holy Spirit. It was in that astonishing encounter that the Lord gave me the assignment to teach third-heaven authority to His people. He also told me that spiritual encounters were going to increase from that point forward. I understood that part of that increase would be connected to spiritual gifts and how believers' use of them would grow exponentially as we draw closer to Jesus' return.

There is no way to overemphasize the importance of embracing our spiritual giftings. God gives gifts for a purpose, and He wants us to use them. That's why Paul encouraged us to "earnestly desire the spiritual gifts" (1 Cor. 14:1, ESV). Part of earnestly desiring is studying and learning. The more we dig into what spiritual gifting is all about, the more we discover about the Holy Spirit's amazing presence. We also begin to understand the specific ways the Spirit reveals things to us personally and how He spiritually energizes us as He flows miraculously through our lives.

Our inner spirits are built with inherent perceptions about the spiritual things in our midst. Just as we live in the natural realm and are aware of what is around us, so we live in the spiritual realm and are aware of things there. However, it is the indwelling Holy Spirit who infuses us with His energies and makes us *super*natural and highly spiritual, infinitely greater than we could be without Him.

CONCERNING SPIRITUAL GIFTS

Let's begin our study of spiritual gifts by looking at Paul's first letter to the Corinthians. The church at Corinth was mostly comprised of Gentiles who were fascinated by the supernatural aspects of the Christian life. As an apostle to the Gentiles, Paul experienced more than his share of spiritual manifestations. To keep the Corinthians' zeal and ignorance from leading them into fleshly behaviors, Paul felt it was necessary to properly instruct them. He knew what he was talking about when he wrote, "Now concerning spiritual gifts, brethren, I do not want you to be ignorant" (1 Cor. 12:1).

So what are spiritual gifts? In this passage the Greek word for *spiritual* is *pneumatikos*, which refers to things involving spiritual essence. Being an adjective, *pneumatikos* was also used in the New Testament to describe concepts such as spiritual blessings, spiritual songs, and spiritual sacrifices (Eph. 1:3; Col. 3:16; 1 Pet. 2:5). According to Vine's Expository Dictionary, *pneumatikos* "always connotes the ideas of invisibility and of power."[1] The things of the Spirit are invisible in the physical realm, but as we've seen, they manifest in physical displays of God's power. Referencing 1 Corinthians 12:1, the dictionary entry also states about believers, "Their appointed activities in the churches are also called 'spiritual gifts,' lit., 'spiritualities.'"[2] Spiritualities are spiritual realities and activities that include the ways of the Spirit. The Bible in Basic English translation picks up on this idea, saying, "About the things of the spirit, my brothers, it is not right for you to be without teaching" (1 Cor. 12:1).

The word *gifts* appears in most English translations of 1 Corinthians 12:1, including the New King James Version. Yet these translations usually note that the word is not found in the original Greek text. Albert Barnes concurs with this by saying, "The word 'gifts' is not in the original. The Greek refers to 'spiritual' things in general, or to anything that is of a spiritual nature. The whole discussion, however, shows that [Paul] refers to the various endowments, gifts, or graces that had been bestowed in different degrees on the members of the church."[3] Translators inserted *gifts* to describe the spiritualities that Paul referenced. They rightfully borrowed the word from verse 4, which reveals that Paul's subject was gifts.

Paul often used the Greek word for *gift*—*charisma*. Vincent's Word Studies defines *charismata*, the plural of *charisma*, as "special endowments of supernatural energy."[4] Interestingly, the Amplified Bible, Classic Edition uses this wording in verse 1: "Now about the spiritual gifts (the special endowments of supernatural energy), brethren, I do not want you to be misinformed."

Spiritual endowments of supernatural energies are granted to us as children of God to enlighten and empower us in every situation. Please understand we are saved by grace alone, not works. There's nothing we can do to earn right standing with God. His gifts are gifts of grace, and they are freely bestowed as add-ons to the supernatural walks we already have with Him. He feels that we need more, and He has designed a way to infuse us with spiritual gifts that equip us to do what we could never do ourselves. God simply wants to partner with us.

Did you know that the entire Godhead—the Father, the Son, and the Holy Spirit—is involved in the endowment of spiritual gifts? Paul continued his teaching in 1 Corinthians 12 by revealing how all this works.

> There are diversities of gifts, but *the same Spirit*. There are differences of ministries, but *the same Lord*. And there are diversities of activities, but it is *the same God* who works all in all. But the manifestation of the Spirit is given to each one for the profit of all.
>
> —1 CORINTHIANS 12:4–7

The Holy Spirit oversees the variety of spiritual endowments that we call the Charismatic gifts (which we will explore in the next chapter). Paul said the displays of the Spirit's indwelling presence are for every believer, in order to work for the good of all. No believer is left out. The great news is that everyone has the Spirit and an accompanying mix of spiritual gifts.

The Trinity's involvement in spiritual gifts is seen in all three types of gifts that we will cover here and in chapter 8.

1. The Holy Spirit oversees the *Charismatic gifts* (which we will cover last).

2. The Father oversees the *motive gifts*.

3. Jesus, the Son, oversees a variety of spiritual ministries, including what we call the *five-fold ministry office gifts*.

MOTIVE GIFTS

Much as the Holy Spirit oversees the Charismatic gifts, so the Father oversees the variety of ways spiritual energies work to accomplish His purposes through us. These ways include what we call the motive gifts. Once our spirits come alive through the new birth, our heavenly Father gives us special abilities that form our spiritual bents in and approaches to life. You could say that these special abilities determine the color of the lenses through which we view life's events and help us then decide how to respond. They are the spiritual motives that make us tick, and Paul covered them in his letter to the Romans.

> For I say, through the grace given to me, to everyone who is among you, not to think of himself more highly than he ought to think, but to think soberly, as God has dealt to each one a measure of faith.... Having then gifts differing according to the grace that is given to us, let us use them: if *prophecy*, let us prophesy in proportion to our faith; or *ministry*, let us use it in our ministering; he who teaches, in *teaching*; he who exhorts, in *exhortation*; he who

> *gives*, with liberality; he who *leads*, with diligence;
> he who shows *mercy*, with cheerfulness.
>
> —ROMANS 12:3, 6–8

Notice how Paul indicated that God Himself oversees these spiritual gifts. The nature of each gift you receive is unique to your relationship with whoever gives it to you. God is the Father, and we are His children. We are family and have been born into His kingdom with aspects of His spiritual DNA. These gifts aren't physical attributes like talents, abilities, and personalities; they are spiritual energies that consecrate those attributes and make them available for God's use. The motive gifts, however, shape our spiritual bents or motivations. Consider this proverb: "Train up a child in the way he should go [and in keeping with his individual gift or bent], and when he is old he will not depart from it" (Prov. 22:6, AMPC). Each of us has our specific bents.

Following are my working definitions of the seven motive gifts Paul mentioned, along with biblical examples and words of caution that apply to each. The definitions are consistent with Scripture, but I'm phrasing them in ways that emphasize their motivational natures. This is not an exhaustive list, but I think Paul figured we would get the idea and would then trust what the heavenly Father would do in us. Please note that on this motivational level the gifts manifest a bit differently than on the other levels. I will explain what this means in greater detail a little later.

1. Prophecy
This is the spiritual predisposition to speak forth from spiritual revelation and spiritual discernment. Prophecy is usually vocal and heavy on revelation or discernment or

both. It is also a vehicle gift, meaning that other gifts can supply the revelation that is being spoken.

When hearing the word *prophecy*, most people immediately think of seeing into the future. An aspect of that is involved. However, foretelling is a combination of other gifts flowing through prophecy. In my experience prophetic people live close to the spiritual realm, making them more sensitive to spiritual things.

Biblical example: When the apostles needed help with the daily administration to the people's needs, one of the men they chose to help was Stephen. He was tuned in to the Spirit at a gut level, making him predisposed to hearing the Spirit and speaking with wisdom and power.

> Stephen, full of faith and power, did great wonders
> and signs among the people....And they were not able
> to resist the wisdom and the Spirit by which he spoke.
>
> —ACTS 6:8, 10

Caution: The more prophetic a person is, the more aware he or she is of demonic activity and oppression. Such people must develop strong senses of faith and authority in order to deal with evil influences. These believers see and feel in the Spirit more profoundly than other people typically do, so they are often accused of reading too much into situations. Yet because of their heightened discernments, they see and address not only circumstances but also spirits, influences, and motivations that are behind circumstances.

2. Ministry

Ministry is the spiritual predisposition for practical service. Those who have this gift approach situations with the ability to see what needs to be done in order to achieve the greatest spiritual benefit. They can be good organizers and tend to be involved with helps ministries in churches, in prophetic or evangelistic ministries, or in other Christian gatherings.

Biblical example: Martha, the sister of Lazarus and Mary, saw the practical ways she and her family would need to care for Jesus' physical needs. Jesus appreciated her service because meeting His physical needs was important. He corrected Martha only when she let her serving stir up strife and get in the way of other people's spiritual needs.

> Now it happened as they went that He entered a certain village; and a certain woman named Martha welcomed Him into her house....But Martha was distracted with much serving.
>
> —Luke 10:38, 40

Caution: Those involved in practical service can experience higher rates of discouragement and burnout than those with other gifts. People with the gift of ministry rarely receive recognition or appreciation that is equal to their services, and they are susceptible to feeling as if others are taking advantage of them. The secret to keeping a good attitude in these situations is remembering that ministry is service to God, not people.

3. Teaching

Teaching is the spiritual predisposition to share scriptural truths with others. These believers love to study God's Word and meditate on the Scriptures. They become excited about revelations the Holy Spirit opens to them, and they want others to know what those revelations are. They frequently steer conversations toward the Bible because they understand that Jesus is the Word and that you can't talk about Him without talking about His Word.

Biblical example: Apollos, Aquila, and Priscilla were passionate about understanding God's Word and teaching scriptural truths to others.

> Now a certain Jew named Apollos, born at Alexandria, an eloquent man and mighty in the Scriptures, came to Ephesus. This man had been instructed in the way of the Lord; and being fervent in spirit, he spoke and taught accurately the things of the Lord, though he knew only the baptism of John. So he began to speak boldly in the synagogue. When Aquila and Priscilla heard him, they took him aside and explained to him the way of God more accurately.
>
> —ACTS 18:24–26

Caution: Believers with the gift of teaching can become frustrated by what seems illogical to them. This includes creative, right-brained people whom they consider to be disorganized in their spiritual lives and undisciplined in the Word. Because this attitude leads to strife and offenses, those with a teaching bent need to pursue ways of relating to a wide variety of people while maintaining a spirit of humility. It is possible for them to develop deeper fellowship in the Word with friends whose giftings are similar to theirs, but they must realize that ministry is the goal when sharing the Word.

In all fairness the tendency to judge others through the lens of one's own gifts and anointing is not limited to those with the teaching gift. It is a problem for many believers, whatever their giftings are.

4. Exhortation

Exhortation is the spiritual predisposition for encouraging others and stimulating their faith. People with this gift usually have a positive view of life and an uncanny ability to see the good that Jesus can do, even in the darkest situations. People are drawn to these encouragers who cause others to feel noticed, cared about, uplifted, and strengthened in their faith.

Biblical example: One such exhorter and encourager in the Bible is Barnabas, whom the apostles relied upon to strengthen believers in the churches.

> And Joses…was also named Barnabas by the apostles (which is translated Son of Encouragement).
>
> —ACTS 4:36

> Then news of these things came to the ears of the church in Jerusalem, and they sent out Barnabas to go as far as Antioch. When he came and had seen the grace of God, he was glad, and encouraged them all that with purpose of heart they should continue with the Lord.
>
> —ACTS 11:22–23

Caution: Exhorters seldom receive the kind of support they give to others. They find it hard to understand why other people don't recognize that encouragers need to also be encouraged, if only with a simple acknowledgment or thank-you. People with this gift get most of their encouragement from the Lord and need to avoid the trap of manipulating those around them into noticing their encouragement needs. They also need to avoid going so deep into other people's problems that they become weighed down and can't see a solution or a way out.

5. Giving

This gift is the spiritual predisposition for earning money to finance the work of the Lord. Believers gifted in this way go beyond the love of helping others in times of need (something all good-hearted believers should be doing). Givers have an unusual, God-given drive to develop ways of making money and then to use that money to finance ministry.

Biblical example: Lydia was a business owner who was known for using her resources to help Paul and Silas in their ministry.

> Now a certain woman named Lydia heard us. She was a seller of purple from the city of Thyatira, who worshiped God. The Lord opened her heart to heed the things spoken by Paul. And when she and her household were baptized, she begged us, saying, "If you have judged me to be faithful to the Lord, come to my house and stay."
>
> —Acts 16:14–15

Caution: Believers with this gift must guard against becoming so immersed in moneymaking that their spiritual and family lives suffer. Another danger they must avoid is thinking that their support buys them a say in the ministries they help finance.

6. Leading

This is the spiritual predisposition to lead with vision and organizational skill. Leadership on this level comes naturally to people with this motive gift. They inspire in others the confidence to unite and work toward specific goals. Their personal characters and strengths are great assets as they serve.

Biblical example: Paul trusted Titus' ability to set into order the leadership structure of various churches.

> To Titus, a true son in our common faith: Grace, mercy, and peace from God the Father and the Lord Jesus Christ our Savior. For this reason I left you in Crete, that you should set in order the things that are lacking, and appoint elders in every city as I commanded you.
>
> —TITUS 1:4–5

Caution: Leaders need to avoid two main pitfalls. The first one is becoming a tyrant who selfishly uses others for his or her own purposes. That's called *abuse*. The second is becoming a people pleaser who appears weak, is influenced by pressure, and is wishy-washy. That is also abusive to those who trust you.

7. Mercy

Mercy is the spiritual predisposition of empathy for other people's distresses. Believers with this gift live close to their own hearts, making them sensitive to other people's problems, including the emotional traumas people face. Those with the mercy motive gift are compassionate by nature and can relate to other people and their difficulties without glossing over situations. They minister to the hearts of those who are hurting and need inner strength.

Biblical example: Empathy and compassion are major topics in Scripture. Jesus was compassionate. In His parable of the good Samaritan it was the Samaritan who "had compassion" for the wounded man (Luke 10:33). Tabitha also appears to be a good example of this motivational gift. She was so loved by the people that Peter was called to raise her from the dead.

> At Joppa there was a certain disciple named Tabitha, which is translated Dorcas. This woman was full of good works and charitable deeds which she did.
>
> —Acts 9:36

Caution: Believers with this gift are sometimes drawn too deeply into other people's needs and problems, as though everyone's troubles were their own. A false sense of responsibility can cause them to lose sight of the big picture. Therefore, they need to remind themselves that they are vessels of the Holy Spirit and not saviors.

Fivefold Ministry Office Gifts

Now let's look at the *fivefold ministry office gifts* that Jesus, the Son, administers. Paul made it clear that the motive gifts and the Charismatic gifts are endowments for all believers. However, the fivefold ministry office gifts are in a different category. While acknowledging these special abilities that Jesus gives to some believers, Paul considered people themselves to be Jesus' gifts to the body of

Christ. He wrote that "His gifts were [varied; He Himself appointed and gave men to us]" (Eph. 4:11, AMPC).

Another difference with this group of gifts is that not every believer has (or is) an office gift. The Contemporary English Version addresses this idea by saying, "Christ *chose some of us to be* apostles, prophets, missionaries, pastors, and teachers" (Eph. 4:11). Paul further amplified these gifts as offices of ministry, writing, "Inasmuch then as I am an apostle to the Gentiles, I lay great stress on my ministry and magnify my office" (Rom. 11:13, AMPC).

Jesus is the Lord and head of the church, and the office gifts help Him oversee and equip His church (Eph. 4:12). So what exactly are the fivefold ministry office gifts? A brief verse lists them.

> He Himself gave some to be *apostles*, some *prophets*, some *evangelists*, and some *pastors* and *teachers*.
>
> —EPHESIANS 4:11

Following are my working definitions for each office gift. As you read through them, please keep a few things in mind. Although these gifts are recognized by man, they are set in the church by Jesus and carry supervisory authority in the church. The other spiritual gifts do not carry this authority, except when it is delegated to them by the presiding office gift. The emphases of the fivefold gifts are placed on office and function, meaning their titles are to be honored, but believers are required to respond to only the spirit of ministry that is in operation.

The apostle

The title *apostle* speaks of a minister who is compelled to go forth, extend the work of the church in new areas and new ways, and then oversee that work.

Biblical example: Jesus chose twelve special apostles for the Jews.

> Now the names of the twelve apostles are these: first, Simon, who is called Peter, and Andrew his brother; James the son of Zebedee, and John his brother; Philip and Bartholomew; Thomas and Matthew the tax collector; James the son of Alphaeus, and Lebbaeus, whose surname was Thaddaeus; Simon the Cananite, and Judas Iscariot, who also betrayed Him.
>
> —MATTHEW 10:2–4

Biblical example: After Judas betrayed Jesus, the remaining eleven apostles prayed and then chose his replacement.

> They prayed and said, "You, O Lord, who know the hearts of all, show which of these two You have chosen to take part in this ministry and apostleship from which Judas by transgression fell, that he might go to his own place." And they cast their lots, and the lot fell on *Matthias*. And he was numbered with the eleven apostles.
>
> —ACTS 1:24–26

Biblical example: Paul, formerly known as Saul, became a special apostle to the Gentiles. He wrote:

> For I speak to you Gentiles; inasmuch as I am an
> apostle to the Gentiles.
>
> —ROMANS 11:13

Biblical example: Two of at least ten other general
apostles are mentioned in Scripture.

> But when the apostles Barnabas and Paul heard this,
> they tore their clothes and ran in among the multi-
> tude, crying out.
>
> —ACTS 14:14

> But I saw none of the other apostles except James,
> the Lord's brother.
>
> —GALATIANS 1:19

The prophet

A prophet is a minister gifted to proclaim to the church
prophetic messages that warn, exhort, and comfort believers.

Biblical example: According to the Book of Acts, the
prophets Judas and Silas spiritually exhorted the church,
and a prophet named Agabus foretold future events.

> Judas and Silas, themselves being prophets also,
> exhorted and strengthened the brethren with many
> words.
>
> —ACTS 15:32

> As we stayed many days, a certain prophet named
> Agabus came down from Judea. When he had come
> to us, he took Paul's belt, bound his own hands and
> feet, and said, "Thus says the Holy Spirit, 'So shall

the Jews at Jerusalem bind the man who owns this belt, and deliver him into the hands of the Gentiles.'"

—Acts 21:10–11

The evangelist

The evangelist is a minister who preaches the gospel with drive and purpose in order to add new converts to the church.

Biblical example: Philip was called an evangelist, and Paul told Pastor Timothy to do the work of an evangelist.

> On the next day we who were Paul's companions departed and came to Caesarea, and entered the house of Philip the evangelist, who was one of the seven, and stayed with him.
>
> —Acts 21:8

> But you [Timothy] be watchful in all things, endure afflictions, do the work of an evangelist, fulfill your ministry.
>
> —2 Timothy 4:5

The pastor

A pastor is a minister who shepherds a flock (a congregation), overseeing, nurturing, and spiritually feeding the people.

Biblical example: The term *pastor*, which means shepherd, is used only in Ephesians 4:11 for this particular office of ministry, which perhaps is why it stuck as a predominant title. Elsewhere in the Bible the terms *elder* and *bishop* are used interchangeably for the same ministry. *Pastor* refers to the love and care required in shepherding a flock. *Elder* characterizes the maturity and wisdom that are needed, and *bishop* points to the necessity of overseeing a whole ministry.

Notice that Peter incorporated all three of these terms when speaking to the same ministers.

> The *elders* who are among you I exhort, I who am a fellow elder and a witness of the sufferings of Christ, and also a partaker of the glory that will be revealed: *Shepherd* [pastor] the flock of God which is among you, serving as *overseers* [bishops], not by compulsion but willingly, not for dishonest gain but eagerly; nor as being lords over those entrusted to you, but being examples to the flock.
>
> —1 PETER 5:1–3

The teacher

A teacher is a minister who instructs believers in biblical truths by clarifying and expounding on the Word of God.

Biblical example: Of the five men named in the following verse, there is no stipulation about which ones were teachers or about whether they all were teachers. It is common for ministers to have more than one office gift, so these ministers were lumped together without further explanation.

> Now in the church that was at Antioch there were certain prophets and teachers: Barnabas, Simeon who was called Niger, Lucius of Cyrene, Manaen who had been brought up with Herod the tetrarch, and Saul.
>
> —ACTS 13:1

Paul was the only one out of the five who later spoke of himself as a teacher, saying, "I was appointed a preacher, an apostle, and a teacher of the Gentiles" (2 Tim. 1:11). A quick note to my learned peers: I have purposefully ignored the discussion of Granville Sharp's rule of connection concerning the nouns *pastor* and *teacher* because it lends nothing to the purpose of this book. Also, a reminder: We'll expound on the Charismatic gifts in the next chapter. I saved them for last because they are at the center of so many supernatural power displays that the Spirit works through believers.

YOUR PERSONAL GIFT MIX

Clearly, an understanding of spiritual gifts is critical if we are to be as accurate and credible as possible. The more we know, the more powerful we become. So in the remaining sections of this chapter we will cover a variety of principles to help us walk in the Spirit. Let's keep two essential points in mind, however: First, every child of God is born unique. Second, each one's DNA is personal, complex, and fine-tuned. This DNA contributes to an individual's personality, temperament, natural talents, and abilities.

Let's also remember that an individual's combination of physical makeup, spiritual gifts, and anointing adds to their uniqueness. When we are saved, the Holy Spirit consecrates our natural attributes so they can be used for our good and for serving Christ Jesus. *To consecrate* means to set someone or something apart for God. We come to Christ as we are. When we are born again, we don't leave our physical lives behind; we bring our physical lives into His kingdom with us.

Paul said it this way:

> I beseech you therefore, brethren, by the mercies of God, that you present your bodies a living sacrifice, holy, acceptable to God, which is your reasonable service. And do not be conformed to this world, but be transformed by the renewing of your mind, that you may prove what is that good and acceptable and perfect will of God.
>
> —Romans 12:1–2

Here's how it works: The Holy Spirit consecrates our natural talents and abilities. The Father layers on His motive gifts. The Holy Spirit then adds another layer of Charismatic gifts. Finally, Jesus chooses who receives the fivefold ministry office gifts. The spiritual gifts we receive transcend our natural abilities, bring us into God's supernatural realm, and allow us to become bigger than we are without them. The gift combinations are limitless, but each believer's personal gift mix is a unique blend.

Bits of Wisdom

Misunderstandings tend to surface when believers discuss spiritual giftings, perhaps because we overlook certain details or are reticent to ask too many questions. The following points may answer some previously unasked questions and open the door to deeper study and understanding.

- No matter how gifted and powerful a believer becomes through the motive and Charismatic gifts, these gifts are not equivalent to the fivefold ministry office gifts in terms of the responsibility and authority they carry in the church. It is said of those in ministry, "Let the elders who rule well be counted worthy of double honor, especially those who labor in the word and doctrine" (1 Tim. 5:17).

- The office gifts aren't vocations but are spiritual callings. Years ago I knew a pastor who led a large congregation in a non-Charismatic denomination. According to his public testimony he received Jesus and was baptized in the Holy Spirit about ten years into his pastorate. He explained to his congregation that he had been raised in the church and therefore assumed that he was a Christian. He added that he attended college and became a pastor as a career choice. It took a spiritual encounter to infuse life and spiritual energies into what had been previously a mere vocation. His congregation reported that his transformation was amazing.

- The more skilled you become in the gifts, the more you will sense the Spirit's anointing, which is part of the spiritual energies that empower you. However, the presence of anointing does not automatically grant you permission to act. Experienced believers learn to flow with other ministries and gifts that are at work in a setting. Different groups may have different protocols for the operations of gifts in public meetings. The Holy Spirit doesn't contradict Himself through dueling manifestations. It is important that we are sensitive and honor the setting and flow of the Spirit. "People who speak what God has revealed must control themselves" (1 Cor. 14:32, GW).

HOW TO HANDLE REVELATORY INFORMATION

We also need specific wisdom for handling any revelatory information we receive from the Holy Spirit. Four steps are essential: revelation, interpretation, application, and evaluation.

Revelation

Jesus promised His disciples that "when He, the Spirit of truth, has come, He will guide you into all truth; for He will not speak on His own authority, but whatever He hears He will speak; and He will tell you things to come" (John 16:13). Remember that a revelation is only the beginning. Then you have to ask:

- What have I seen or heard?

- How did it come?

- Do I recognize God's voice or the Lord's form in the revelation?

- Did it cause fear or faith? (God leads only by faith, even in fearful situations.)

- Does it help or hinder my walk with God?

- Is the heart of Father God in it?

- Does it point others toward Jesus? Or am I
  pushing a personal agenda or drawing attention to myself?

Answer these questions honestly. Don't embellish or be too quick to assume what the revelation means. Take the time to be accurate.

Interpretation

When seeking to interpret a revelation, consider this truth: "It is the glory of God to conceal a matter, but the glory of kings is to search out a matter" (Prov. 25:2). What is God saying? Sometimes He gives actual words of knowledge about specific people, places, and things. At other times He uses allegories or parables instead of literal examples.

If you were to have a dream about an earthquake, would it necessarily foretell a literal earthquake? Or might it symbolize the spiritual shaking of a nation, church, or system? Or perhaps it would point to major cracks developing in the walls of a stronghold that God wants to bring down. Also, consider how the dream would hold up to Scripture. Neither a genuine revelation from God nor its accurate interpretation will ever violate His Word. He will, however, violate your personal doctrines at times.

The better you know God's Word, the more the Holy Spirit has to work with. If you're not sure what the Word says about a certain revelation, let your uncertainty drive you into reading the Bible and praying to find out whether the revelation is really from God and what it means.

Application

What, if anything, does God want you to do about what you have heard? A revelation should provide some sense of wisdom and edification. Sometimes God simply puts you on notice with the awareness that He is the initiator concerning the revelation.

> Surely the Lord GOD does nothing, unless He reveals His secret to His servants the prophets.
>
> —AMOS 3:7

Let's say you had a vision of yourself riding in a car. Would God want you to actually get into your car and drive somewhere? Or would the image be about movement, with God possibly instructing you to set something in motion? Maybe the vehicle would represent your ministry, which should carry you (and not the other way around). My point is that you should not assume anything but should pray over the revelation so you can receive greater insight.

When revelation comes, it is important to be in touch with all your perceptions: the emotions that accompanied the experience, the impressions you sensed, and the colors and sounds that caught your attention. All these are pieces of the puzzle and will help you make sense of the mystery. God interacts with you through all your perceptions and emotions. He created them, and the sum of them brings understanding.

Finally, bear in mind that many people miss what God is saying because their doctrines don't allow them to listen to Him with these ideas in mind.

Evaluation

As you proceed, take time to revisit the prophetic word. Further insight will unfold as the Holy Spirit leads you, one step at a time. If you make a mistake, it's OK. Don't be too proud or embarrassed to admit it, and make any necessary corrections. Also, look for patterns in how this revelation and others came to you. That's how you learn the ways God uses your unique personality and individual gift mix. No two people hear God the same way.

An interesting illustration of these principles is found in Paul's ministry. The Holy Spirit impressed upon him a compelling need to go to Jerusalem. He told the elders at Ephesus, "Now I go bound in the spirit to Jerusalem" (Acts 20:22). So off he went, obedient and fully aware of what may happen to him.

On his journey, however, Paul stopped at Philip's house to encourage him and his four daughters, who were prophets. During his visit something noteworthy happened—something so noteworthy that it bears repeating.

> As we stayed many days, a certain prophet named Agabus came down from Judea. When he had come to us, he took Paul's belt, bound his own hands and feet, and said, "Thus says the Holy Spirit, 'So shall the Jews at Jerusalem bind the man who owns this belt, and deliver him into the hands of the Gentiles.'" Now when we heard these things, both we and those from that place pleaded with him not to go up to Jerusalem. Then Paul answered, "What do you mean by weeping and breaking my heart? For I am ready not only to be bound, but also to die at Jerusalem for the name of the Lord Jesus." So when he would not be persuaded, we ceased, saying, "The will of the Lord be done."
>
> —Acts 21:10–14

Agabus and the other prophets heard correctly from the Holy Spirit. They also accurately interpreted the revelation as a warning of trouble ahead. However, their evaluation was off. They assumed that they were supposed to prevent Paul from going where the trouble would be. Paul took issue with their assessment and assured them that going to Jerusalem was the Spirit's idea in the first place.

Agabus and the others misunderstood the Spirit's intent—they thought He wanted Paul to avoid the difficulty. Instead, the Spirit wanted to prepare the churches so they would not be surprised by Paul's arrest. It became their job to pray for him through the ordeal, as the Lord carried him into the next phase of his ministry.

All that we are learning will make us more effective in our personal walks with the Lord, and it will better equip us to fulfill our assignments in the Lion's army. Now, let's move to the next chapter, part 2 of our study on the spiritual gifts, specifically the Charismatic gifts.

Chapter 8

SPIRITUAL GIFTS, PART 2

THE WAYS OF the Holy Spirit are inexhaustible. The third person of the Trinity, God's divine presence within us, is our source of wisdom, revelation, spiritual energies, and power. In addition the Holy Spirit endows us with supernatural abilities as He works through us. We call these abilities the *Charismatic gifts*, and they exceed our natural abilities, even when our natural abilities are consecrated by God.

For example, if the gift of healings meant being a doctor or nurse, then nonbelievers could be said to possess spiritual gifts. While those in the medical field certainly have special natural abilities, great knowledge, and discipline that God uses to benefit humanity, those things aren't spiritual gifts. On the other hand, a plumber, coach, CPA, or chef, or any person in any field or walk of life, can be endowed with amazing spiritual gifts of healings.

A simple ground rule is this: If a person can accomplish something without the Holy Spirit, then it isn't a gift from the Holy Spirit. The word *gift* implies something that is given to you—something you do not possess naturally and did not earn. When the Charismatic gifts are operating in your life, miraculous revelations and power displays occur, revealing the ways of the Spirit. Paul affirmed these gifts in his first letter to the Corinthians.

> To one is given the *word of wisdom* through the Spirit, to another the *word of knowledge* through the same Spirit, to another *faith* by the same Spirit, to another *gifts of healings* by the same Spirit, to another the *working of miracles*, to another *prophecy*, to another *discerning of spirits*, to another *different kinds of tongues*, to another the *interpretation of tongues*. But one and the same Spirit works all these things, distributing to each one individually as He wills.
>
> —1 CORINTHIANS 12:8–11

In this passage we see nine Charismatic gifts that can be divided into three categories of three gifts each. Three gifts give special revelation: the word of wisdom, the word of knowledge, and the discerning of spirits. Three gifts release great power through us: the gift of faith, the gift of healings, and the working of miracles. Finally, three gifts require us to speak: the gift of prophecy, the different kinds of tongues, and the interpretation of tongues.

Over the next several pages I will define each gift, explain how it works, give an example of its use in the Word of God, and give a testimony dealing with that gift. Because there are thousands of testimonies from which to choose, it was difficult to select which ones to share. However, the Spirit impressed specific examples upon my mind.

THE NINE CHARISMATIC GIFTS EXPLAINED

Please note that I have rearranged the order of the Charismatic gifts from their order presented in 1 Corinthians 12. I did this to emphasize the groupings and make the explanations a bit clearer.

1. Word of wisdom

This is special wisdom from the mind of the Spirit that reveals something within God's will. In Scripture we find the three revelation gifts manifesting through visions, dreams, prophecies, and angelic visitations, as well as through heart knowledge or awareness, the inner voice of the Holy Spirit, and the audible voice of God. This is because the Holy Spirit's presence and resulting energies are involved in all spiritual manifestations, including the activities of the Father, Jesus, and angels.

We know that Jesus and the Holy Spirit worked in close collaboration during Jesus' earthly ministry (Acts 10:38), and they continue to do so now that the Lord is in heaven. Angels have often externally orchestrated miracles for believers, but the Holy Spirit empowered believers from the inside (Acts 8:26, 29, 39).

Biblical example: In Acts 10:10–48 Peter received wisdom from the Spirit to embrace Gentiles in the church. The Holy Spirit put Peter in a trance. Then He gave him a vision of the heavens opening and a sheet descending, a sheet filled with "all kinds of four-footed animals of the earth, wild beasts, creeping things, and birds of the air" (Acts 10:12). Even though the vision depicted animals that were considered unclean according to Jewish law, the Lord told Peter to "kill and eat" (v. 13). When he refused, the Lord said, "What God has cleansed you must not call common" (v. 15).

Immediately, the Spirit sent Peter to preach salvation to a Gentile named Cornelius and to those in Cornelius' household. The Holy Spirit gave Peter the wisdom to see that Jesus died for all and that Gentiles who put their faith in the Lord were made clean. Peter then declared, "In truth I perceive that God shows no partiality. But in every nation whoever fears Him and works righteousness is accepted by Him" (vv. 34–35; see also vv. 19–33).

Biblical example: Paul received specific wisdom and direction directly from the Spirit concerning his steps in personal ministry. The Spirit even prevented him from ministering in a place called Bithynia.

> Now when they had gone through Phrygia and the region of Galatia, they were forbidden by the Holy Spirit to preach the word in Asia. After they had come to Mysia, they tried to go into Bithynia, but the Spirit did not permit them. So passing by Mysia, they came down to Troas. And a vision appeared to Paul in the night. A man of Macedonia stood and pleaded with him, saying, "Come over to Macedonia and help us." Now after he had seen the vision, immediately we sought to go to Macedonia, concluding that the Lord had called us to preach the gospel to them.
>
> —ACTS 16:6–10

Personal testimony: In 2013 CK and I began to feel stirrings in our hearts about a change that was coming to our ministry. Not knowing what the change was, we decided to take a sabbatical to seek the Lord at His will. Our ministry was headquartered in Oregon at the time, so our time-share in Las Vegas seemed like the best place to get away to.

One morning CK and I prayed separately; she was in the bedroom, and I was in the living room. As CK was praying in English and tongues, so I was when I suddenly felt a strong anointing come over me, and I was pulled into a vision. During the encounter I was raised high over the continental United States and witnessed a great rainbow cloud of God's glory being lowered onto the nation.

The archangel Michael interacted with me for a while about the meaning of the vision. As the encounter seemed to wind down (and to my utter surprise), Michael looked straight at me and said, "You may fulfill your ministry assignment from any location that you choose. However, the Lord would rather have you do it from here!"

You could have knocked me over with a feather! The angel was telling me that it was time for the next step and that we could relocate our ministry to the place of our choosing. The Lord would honor whatever choice we made, but He preferred Las Vegas.

CK and I immediately prayed about this and felt led to move our ministry headquarters to Las Vegas. Interestingly, the location of our house and studio now is directly in the line of sight of the time-share window I was looking through when the vision occurred.

2. Word of knowledge

The word of knowledge is special knowledge from the mind of the Spirit concerning natural facts.

Biblical example: When Jesus met the Samaritan woman at the well, He knew by the Spirit what her marital history was before she confirmed it.

> Jesus said to her, "Go, call your husband, and come here." The woman answered and said, "I have no husband." Jesus said to her, "You have well said, 'I have no husband,' for you have had five husbands, and the one whom you now have is not your husband; in that you spoke truly." The woman said to Him, "Sir, I perceive that You are a prophet."
>
> —John 4:16–19

Biblical example: An angel appeared to give instructions to a devout Gentile named Cornelius, whom I mentioned earlier. The angel provided information, including the physical information he would need and could not have known by any other means. The angel said:

> Now send men to Joppa, and send for Simon whose surname is Peter. He is lodging with Simon, a tanner, whose house is by the sea. He will tell you what you must do.
>
> —Acts 10:5–6

Personal testimony: CK and I had been in full-time ministry only a few months when we held a meeting in Coos Bay, Oregon. The location was a public banquet room, and the teaching anointing was heavy on me as I delivered a penetrating message about the miraculous power of God. While I was preaching, the Spirit kept drawing my attention to a woman who was seated toward the rear of the audience. I had no idea why I was made so keenly aware of her.

After ending my message, I openly told the woman that the Holy Spirit had highlighted her to me. Then I asked her if she needed prayer. She stood up and somewhat skeptically said (as if to prove whether I was legit), "If the Lord can show you that I need prayer, then He can tell you what I need prayer for."

Talk about putting me on the spot! I wasn't sure how to handle the situation, but I believed that the Holy Spirit had the answer. So I said under my breath, "Holy Spirit, You put me in this situation, and You're going to have to get me out of it. Since I still feel Your anointing on my speech, I'm going to open my mouth and let You fill it with prophetic words."

Then I heard myself say these words to the woman: "You came tonight because your teenage daughter ran away from home a few days ago and you are at your wit's end with fear and concern. The Lord says that you haven't heard from her but you will very soon. She is safe, and she will be back home in a day or two."

I don't know who was more shocked, me or the woman. By that time, she was sobbing and had fallen back into her chair. She looked at me and said, "Man of God, that is exactly what happened. Now I can go home in faith and wait for my daughter's return." The next day she sent me word through a mutual friend that her daughter had just called and was on her way home.

3. Discerning of spirits

This is special insight from the mind of the Spirit that allows you to distinguish and judge the nature of spiritual entities. This spiritual discernment pertains to all spirit beings: angels, demons, and human spirits, as well as the Holy Spirit. Some misunderstand this gift as a license to be judgmental or critical, but it is not. When the discerning of spirits is in operation, you sense the existence of spiritual influences behind physical events and then judge whether their origins and natures are godly.

Biblical example: Paul discerned and cast out a spirit of divination from a girl. The girl did not say anything untrue, but the source of her information was demonic. That means her agenda was to deceptively draw attention to herself. Luke described the encounter this way:

> Now it happened, as we went to prayer, that a certain slave girl possessed with a spirit of divination met us, who brought her masters much profit by fortune-telling. This girl followed Paul and us, and cried out, saying, "These men are the servants of the Most High God, who proclaim to us the way of salvation." And this she did for many days.
>
> But Paul, greatly annoyed, turned and said to the spirit, "I command you in the name of Jesus Christ to come out of her." And he came out that very hour.
>
> —ACTS 16:16–18

Biblical example: Joseph, the husband of Jesus' mother, Mary, accurately discerned that the angel in his dream was from God and was not a demonic deception. He then acted in faith to obey God's leading, which Matthew's Gospel describes.

> Now when they had departed, behold, an angel of the Lord appeared to Joseph in a dream, saying, "Arise, take the young Child and His mother, flee to Egypt, and stay there until I bring you word; for Herod will seek the young Child to destroy Him."
>
> —MATTHEW 2:13

Personal testimony: Over the years, I've discerned demonic spirits in many ways, but the story I'm about to share is perhaps the most bizarre. I can assure you that it happened, however.

After we moved to Las Vegas, I was invited to preach in a church back in Oregon. The building was packed, and a feeling of expectation was in the air. As we worshipped, I remembered that I had left something in the car, so I slipped out to retrieve it. With the item in hand, I headed back across the church parking lot.

A few people were coming and going, but one man standing outside the door caught my attention. Something about him seemed a little off, but nothing could have prepared me for what happened next. As I passed by him, his head turned into a cartoon-like figure that ballooned straight out toward me with a hideous, threatening glare. I realized that I was discerning the presence of a demon that had driven the man to attempt to disrupt the service. CK had once described her experience with this type of manifestation, but this was a first for me.

Knowing that worship was ending and the pastor would soon introduce me as the guest speaker, I continued going back to my seat inside. Entering the door, I pointed out the man to an usher and said, "That man has a demon, and he's come to disrupt today's service. Don't let him in."

I presume the man wasn't allowed to come in and cause any problems, because I didn't see him again. I was on the platform for the rest of the service.

4. Gift of faith

Notice that I have added the words *gift of* here. I did so because this is not the baseline of faith that we have in God for salvation and for serving Him. The gift of faith is what I call an add-on gift. It is imparted by the Spirit during specific times of ministry or trial that require the shoring up of one's faith.

Biblical example: Similar to the threats to Daniel in the lions' den and to the three faithful Hebrews cast into the fiery furnace by Nebuchadnezzar (Dan. 6:10–23; 3:8–25), the opposition our Lord faced in the Garden of Gethsemane brought Him to a place of complete collapse (Matt. 26:36–46). His agony was so great that He sweat drops of blood (Luke 22:44). This is a rare, extreme medical phenomenon known as *hematidrosis*.[1] Yet in that crushing moment, Jesus received from the Holy Spirit the special sustaining faith that held Him steady as an angel strengthened Him.

> Then Jesus came with them to a place called Gethsemane, and said to the disciples, "Sit here while I go and pray over there." And He took with Him Peter and the two sons of Zebedee, and He began to be sorrowful and deeply distressed. Then

He said to them, "My soul is exceedingly sorrowful, even to death. Stay here and watch with Me."

—MATTHEW 26:36–38

Now an angel from heaven appeared to Him, strengthening Him. And being in agony, He was praying very fervently; and His sweat became like drops of blood, falling down upon the ground.

—LUKE 22:43–44, NASB

Biblical example: Paul experienced many difficult periods in his ministry. At one point the persecution was so intense that he felt as though a lion was threatening to tear him apart. Yet he was supernaturally strengthened with faith to carry on and be victorious.

At my first defense no one stood with me, but all forsook me. May it not be charged against them.

But the Lord stood with me and strengthened me, so that the message might be preached fully through me, and that all the Gentiles might hear. Also I was delivered out of the mouth of the lion. And the Lord will deliver me from every evil work and preserve me for His heavenly kingdom. To Him be glory forever and ever. Amen!

—2 TIMOTHY 4:16–18

Personal testimony: One of the times when I genuinely felt an anointing of faith come upon me was when I was a young minister. While I preached one of my first sermons, the doors to the sanctuary opened, and two people came in pushing a wheelchair that carried a middle-aged man. Though I considered myself a bold preacher, something got hold of me and tormented me for the rest of the sermon. The devil—that liar and accuser—whispered in my ear the whole time, saying things such as, "They brought that man to be healed today. You've never prayed for someone in a wheelchair before. You don't have the faith or power to produce a miracle. You are going to fail miserably in front of everyone."

I dreaded the end of my message because it meant I would soon have to face the music. Not knowing what to do, I whispered to Jesus that no matter how hard it was, I was going to obey His Word and pray for the sick. I finished my sermon and asked the congregation, "Would anyone like to receive prayer for healing today?"

Several people responded with raised hands, including those who had brought the man in the wheelchair. I had given the invitation by *my* faith, but suddenly an anointing for the *gift of* faith hit me so strongly that I felt not only boldness but anger at the devil. I walked straight toward the front of the wheelchair, laid my hands on the gentleman, and decreed, "Be healed in Jesus' name."

As I spoke, I raised the man out of his chair, and he was healed by the power of God. He started walking around and praising God. His friends praised God too. It was an obvious miracle.

5. Gifts of healings

This is a special endowment of power to remove sicknesses and diseases. As believers we have an inherent right to pray for healing at any time. However, the Holy Spirit also anoints certain believers with specific powers for healing. For instance, one person might be highly anointed to pray for those with cancer, while another is particularly gifted to pray for the inner healing of people's hearts. Someone else might have a public ministry of remarkable miracles and astounding healings. These are all examples of the Charismatic gift of healings.

Biblical example: A curious passage from Acts chapter 5 says that the miracles performed by the apostles in Jerusalem were so numerous that people brought the sick in hopes that Peter's shadow may touch and heal them. Critics point out that the narrative doesn't attribute any specific miracle to Peter's shadow, but the narrative does not deny that such a miracle happened. What is obvious from the text is a spiritual atmosphere ripe with special manifestations of healings.

> Through the hands of the apostles many signs and wonders were done among the people. And they were all with one accord in Solomon's Porch....They brought the sick out into the streets and laid them on beds and couches, that at least the shadow of Peter passing by might fall on some of them. Also a multitude gathered from the surrounding cities to Jerusalem, bringing sick people and those who were tormented by unclean spirits, and they were all healed.
>
> —ACTS 5:12, 15–16

Biblical example: Paul was gifted to perform special miracles involving pieces of fabric that he handled.

> Now God worked unusual miracles by the hands of Paul, so that even handkerchiefs or aprons were

brought from his body to the sick, and the diseases
left them and the evil spirits went out of them.

—ACTS 19:11–12

I would like to point out right here that the same Holy
Spirit who worked in the apostles is working in us as
believers. And the same Charismatic gifts that operated
then are operating today—in us.

Personal testimony: Years ago, at the direction of our
Lord Jesus, the Holy Spirit gave me a special gift of healings. I was in my car, enjoying some alone time with the
Lord while driving to preach in another city. I'd been
praying in the Spirit (tongues) for about an hour when an
anointing filled the car, and the Spirit began speaking to
me prophetically. At first I was confused because before
that this specific anointing had come onto me only when I
was in a gathering of believers. I fully recognized the type
of anointing, but the context was new to me.

Opening my mouth to speak, I heard myself uttering
these words from the Lord: "Up until now the anointing
for bodily healing has been on your ministry. From this
day forward, you will also carry the anointing for the
healing and restoring of people's hearts. Many will experience inner healings by sitting under your ministry."

It was an amazing experience, and from that day forward, people began receiving wonderful healings in their
souls through my ministry. It should be noted that such
healings can be associated with the removal of demonic
spirits and the miraculous restoration of the body. (See
Acts 5:16 and Luke 17:12–19.)

6. Working of miracles

The working of miracles is the special power to alter natural laws.

Biblical example: Jesus miraculously multiplied a small amount of bread and fish so that it would feed five thousand men, plus thousands of women and children who were present with them.

> When He had taken the five loaves and the two fish, He looked up to heaven, blessed and broke the loaves, and gave them to His disciples to set before them; and the two fish He divided among them all. So they all ate and were filled. And they took up twelve baskets full of fragments and of the fish. Now those who had eaten the loaves were about five thousand men.
>
> —MARK 6:41–44

Biblical example: Perhaps following Elisha's example of raising a child from the dead in 2 Kings 4:32–37, Paul was able to restore life to a young man who died in an accident.

> In a window sat a certain young man named Eutychus, who was sinking into a deep sleep. He was overcome by sleep; and as Paul continued speaking, he fell down from the third story and was taken up dead. But Paul went down, fell on him, and embracing him said, "Do not trouble yourselves, for his life is in him."...And they brought the young man in alive, and they were not a little comforted.
>
> —ACTS 20:9–10, 12

Personal testimony: Early in our marriage, long before CK and I went into ministry, both of us were baptized in the Holy Spirit. At the time, we were part of a prayer group that met weekly in my parents' home. All of us were passionately in love with Jesus and full of faith for miracles. On one occasion the group went on a retreat in the mountains. After several days of fellowship with each other and the Holy Spirit, we learned that our group's supply of food would not last the remaining twenty-four hours of our retreat.

No one wanted to make the trip into town to buy groceries for just one day, so we gathered together, full of faith and enthusiasm, and prayed in agreement, asking the Lord to multiply the food. After all, isn't that what Jesus would have done?

The cooks put the last of our provisions together to make that night's spaghetti and side dishes, and the twenty of us (approximately) took turns filling our plates. At first we were careful not to take too much. But soon we realized that there would be enough, and we happily went back for seconds. When dinner was over, the cooks couldn't believe what they saw—there was almost as much food left over as there had been when we started eating. We all thanked the Lord for His goodness and gave honor to the Holy Spirit for multiplying our food.

Sharing this testimony makes me so appreciative of my sweet wife. What a powerhouse CK is for Jesus! From the beginning she has allowed the Spirit to freely move through her, and she is ever ready to believe Him for daily miracles. We have been through fifty years of one divine encounter or spiritual manifestation after another. Even when we endured severe trials, CK was by my side. And Jesus always kept His promises to us.

7. Gift of prophecy

Here I have again added the words *gift of* to differentiate this gift from the motive gift of prophecy, which is a personal prophetic bent. In regard to Charismatic prophecy, it is the ability to speak inspired words in a known language and unveil hidden truths. The gift usually operates in groups of two or more believers. As I mentioned earlier, prophecy is also a vehicle gift that depends on the other Charismatic gifts to supply the spiritual revelations that need to be spoken.

Biblical example: Right after Jesus made His triumphant entry into Jerusalem, some Pharisees demanded that He rebuke His disciples. Instead, Jesus ended up prophesying over the city.

> As He drew near, He saw the city and wept over it, saying, "If you had known, even you, especially in this your day, the things that make for your peace! But now they are hidden from your eyes. For days will come upon you when your enemies will build an embankment around you, surround you and close you in on every side, and level you, and your children within you, to the ground; and they will not leave in you one stone upon another, because you did not know the time of your visitation."
>
> —LUKE 19:41–44

Biblical example: After Paul arrived in Ephesus, he asked some disciples there whether they had received the Holy Spirit (Acts 19:2). Paul then spoke to them, and "they were baptized in the name of the Lord Jesus" (v. 5). Then Paul continued ministering to them, and the gift of prophecy came upon them.

> When Paul had laid hands on them, the Holy Spirit
> came upon them, and they spoke with tongues and
> prophesied. Now the men were about twelve in all.
>
> —ACTS 19:6–7

Personal testimony: The first prophecy I remember giving was for those in a church prayer meeting. It wasn't a personal prophecy spoken to an individual but was a public prophecy given to the whole group. I had been baptized in the Spirit for several months and had witnessed numerous such prophecies given by believers who were more experienced than I was. There was no doubt in my mind concerning God's ability to speak to His people; I just wasn't sure that He would use me.

During the prayer time I noticed that a few words kept running through my head. They seemed to be words that God would use to encourage someone. However, it was just one sentence that didn't make a complete thought. Along with the words, I felt a new sensation. It was as if the Holy Spirit wanted me to open my mouth and let Him say something. I had to talk, but I didn't want to.

The sensation wouldn't quit. Toward the end of the meeting, when everyone was winding down their prayers, a peaceful silence filled the room, and I couldn't resist any longer. In faith I opened my mouth to let the Spirit flow out, and I spoke the sentence that had been playing over in my head. To my surprise a flood of sentences from my mouth followed the first one until the whole message was delivered. What I spoke was an uplifting word of encouragement from the Lord, and everyone seemed to accept it as such. Having prophesied that way once, I realized I could do it again whenever I recognized the Spirit's presence on me that way.

8. Different kinds of tongues

This gift and the next are closely related and work together. The gift of different kinds of tongues is the ability to speak inspired words in a language not known by the speaker. This gift is intended to operate with the next gift, the interpretation of tongues. I am listing the two gifts separately but will provide an explanation, a biblical example, and a personal testimony for both *after* I list the next gift.

9. Interpretation of tongues

The interpretation of tongues is the ability to speak inspired words that interpret, or translate, different kinds of tongues into a known language that can profit the hearers.

Working together, different kinds of tongues and the interpretation of tongues compose a New Testament spirituality and serve as signs of the Lord's presence with His people (1 Cor. 14:22). They are the only two Charismatic gifts not found in the Old Testament. However, types of these two gifts can be seen in Bible passages such as Daniel 5:5–17, in which the finger of God wrote in an unknown language on King Belshazzar's wall. Only Daniel, a man of God, could interpret what God's finger had written.

Biblical example: Paul validated the significance of these gifts when he gave instructions to the Corinthians for how the gifts should operate in public church services. It's important to note that there is a difference between different kinds of tongues and a believer's own personal prayer language in tongues. The simplest way to explain the difference is to look at Paul's instructions concerning the purposes and directions of the tongues. The Charismatic gift, different kinds of tongues, is God speaking to believers who are gathered in His name so that "with men of other tongues and other lips [He] will speak to [the] people" (1 Cor. 14:21). The message from God is then interpreted for the edification of everyone. Praying in tongues, on the other hand, is a believer speaking to God. Paul wrote of this, saying, "He who speaks in a tongue does not speak to men but to God, for no one understands him; however, in the spirit he speaks mysteries" (1 Cor. 14:2).

Paul also explained that different kinds of tongues and the interpretation of tongues properly working together is equal to prophecy. He wrote, "He who prophesies is greater than he who speaks with tongues, unless indeed he interprets, that the church may receive edification" (1 Cor. 14:5). "Therefore," Paul instructed, "brethren, desire earnestly to prophesy, and do not forbid to speak with tongues" (1 Cor. 14:39).

Personal testimony: CK and I have always felt that in spiritual revelation the combination of tongues and interpretation of tongues is equal to prophecy but with a slight difference: Believers tend to be greatly blessed by prophecy, while tongues and their interpretation really get the attention of unbelievers (1 Cor. 14:22). There was a season in our ministry when the Holy Spirit had us operating together in these two gifts frequently during meetings. Usually, CK gave the tongue and I gave the interpretation.

One Sunday, when we were about to start our service, a middle-aged man and his wife entered the sanctuary. He was carrying a briefcase and seemed to be a little wary. He wasn't unpleasant but was perhaps unsure about whether he and his wife were in a safe, credible church. Yet they found a couple of seats among the congregation and sat down. The gentleman opened his briefcase on his lap and removed from it a Bible and notepad, along with another book. By this time, the service had started, and CK was leading worship from her keyboard.

As the worship songs were ending, I walked up front to stand next to CK. A heavy anointing made the atmosphere conducive for us to minister together in the spiritual gifts. Sure enough, CK gave the tongue, and I gave the interpretation. The service proceeded, and throughout my preaching the man kept his nose in his books, intensely jotting down notes.

When the service ended, the man came forward to introduce himself to CK and me. Carrying a handful of papers with him, he said he was a Spirit-filled Messianic rabbi and Greek scholar. He apologized for being so studious during the service and then confessed that he had come to check us out. A friend of his was attending our church, and he wanted to know whether we were flaky or legit.

He continued by telling us that when CK gave the tongue in the meeting, he recognized it as an ancient form of Greek, and he understood what the Spirit said through her. He scribbled the words on his notepad as fast as he could, in English. Then, when I gave the interpretation, he likewise wrote it down on the same page. He handed us his notes and said, "If you read both of them, you will find that while they are not word-for-word duplicates, they are identical thought-for-thought translations. Mike's interpretation perfectly matched what the Spirit said through CK."

Lastly, he told us that he scrutinized my sermon by

consulting both his Bibles—one in English and the other in Greek. He then said, "Mike, your sermon was not only anointed but technically correct. The Bible says what you declared the Bible to say. And your definitions of the Greek words were accurate."

That is how I met Messianic Rabbi Rich Ford. CK and I became close friends with Rich and his wife, Arlene.

MORE BITS OF WISDOM

Let me close this chapter with several important points.

- The spiritual gifts operate individually and in various combinations. Defining each gift helps us better understand the different ways the Holy Spirit energizes us and helps us recognize His leading. When you've been doing this as long as CK and I have, the gifts tend to dovetail, intertwine, and flow together. Over time you learn the ways of the Spirit because He teaches you. The primary requirement is being a willing and credible vessel.

- I'm often asked whether I can move in the gifts anytime I want to. The answer is yes. But there is a qualifier. The gifts are endowments given to me, and they've become part of my spiritual nature. I've had so much experience that I can open myself up anytime and start picking things up in the spiritual realm. The Lord has allowed me to consciously move in the gifts, but I have no control over how the Spirit uses me or what the Spirit shows me. That is the qualifier.

- You could explain it this way: I have a teaching gift and function in the office of a teacher. I don't have to sit around waiting for the gift to kick in so I can then go find someone to whom I can teach spiritual truths. The gifts are mine, and I'm ready to use them anytime. Yet I need the Spirit's inspiration to know what to teach, when to teach, and where to teach. This principle applies to all the gifts.

- How we see the gifts function in church or in other public meetings is not the same as how they function through individual believers in their daily lives. We don't announce to our neighbors that we are going to have a prayer line in our front yard and then line everyone up, lay hands on them, and prophesy and pray for each person. The gifts are spiritual energies that flow through us in more normal ways as we move about our days, from the supermarket to the kids' soccer games.

- In a service I might say to a member, "The Lord just told me to pray for you and release a healing anointing for your back. Come up here, and I'll lay hands on your head. When I do, I want the whole church to shout, 'Release!' with me." When someone visits my home, or when I see someone in a coffee shop, I do it differently. The same gifts are flowing, but I might say more casually, "John, while we've been talking, I've kept getting the impression that your back is bothering you. Is that true? And if it is, can I pray for you? I think God wants to heal you." Then I would lay my hand on his shoulder and pray the prayer of faith in a normal, conversational tone. Faith and obedience, not methodology, are the keys to success.

- No one is a perfect vessel. We all make mistakes. However, there is an imperative for using the gifts. It starts with humility. Paul wrote, "I say, through the grace given to me, to everyone who is among you, not to think of himself more highly than he ought to think, but to think soberly, as God has dealt to each one a measure of faith" (Rom. 12:3). The "measure of faith" you have for spiritual gifting is due to an act of God's grace and should be handled as such. Never use spiritual gifting to manipulate and control others or to narcissistically inflate your stature or importance. The Bible compares this with witchcraft. The graces and powers of the Holy Spirit are gifts of love. They bring liberty to people, not bondage. And the Holy Spirit will bring honor to whom honor is due.

- Operating in the gifts requires faith. We must have faith in the Holy Spirit and in His ability to use us. We must also learn to trust what the Spirit is doing within our hearts, for out of our hearts "spring the issues of life" (Prov. 4:23). How many times have we made the wrong choices only to say, "I knew inside not to do that, but I talked myself out of the truth"?

- Finally, never be afraid of making mistakes, because you will make them, and you will learn from them. The gift is perfect, but the vessel errs at times.

The key to moving in the spiritual gifts is to keep moving forward in faith. The Charismatic gifts we just explored are crucial to every single warrior in the Lion's army. Is it any wonder that the beast wants to shut down these gifts and keep them down?

Chapter 9

A NEW CHRISTIAN ERA

OR THE PAST eight years I've taught that we are living
in a new Christian era. I'm not referring to the New
Covenant (the New Testament) or the church age,
which is the period between Jesus' ascension to heaven
and return to earth—a period of more than two thousand
years so far. I'm also not speaking of the shorter seasons, or
chapters, that we all experience in life. An *era*, in the sense
that I'm using the word, is an interval of time marked by
reformation. It's a changing of the way things have been
done in order to achieve the end result God desires.

In the current new Christian era the Holy Spirit is doing
unprecedented work throughout the body of Christ to
equip and empower it to meet the world's new challenges.
As I write this, I believe we will be in this era for at least
twenty more years, maybe longer. Our jobs as born-again
believers and effective warriors in the Lion's army are to
live with attentive postures, ready to receive equipment
from the Holy Spirit. It's the opposite of living spiritually

lethargic, system-driven religious lives, "having a form of godliness but denying its power" (2 Tim. 3:5).

I say that because in the years following periods of major revival and church growth, there have historically come lulls in spiritual fervor, lulls that allow complacency and ritualism to take root. While the people carrying the fire of the Spirit from the last outpouring begin to decrease in numbers, the generation following them mistakenly thinks it's their job to quell what they consider to be excess or wildfire. Their "logical" conclusion then is to use physical, fleshly means to attempt what only the fire of the Spirit can do.

Consequently, the fire dies out, and dry, stale religion takes its place. Christian worship and services become more and more coordinated and manipulated, and spiritually corrupt. The emphasis on organization seems to increasingly control God's people rather than spiritually equip them to be forces for Jesus. With the fire of the Spirit quelled, the church's effect on the world is stifled.

A fresh outpouring of the Spirit becomes necessary to breathe into the church the new life that revitalizes it. It is described in Scripture as new wine being poured into new wineskins (Matt. 9:17). This is not to be confused with new wine that is poured into old wineskins, causing them to burst. This is about new wine and new wineskins so that spiritual life is welcomed and stirred. Believers become active participants with the Holy Spirit, leading to an overflow of the transforming presence of God in their lives and of the passion to see other lives transformed as well.

With each new outpouring comes a large exodus of believers from controlling, organizational structures. The

Good Shepherd's sheep begin to escape man-made pens to find the freedom and the nourishment of new grass. And why wouldn't they? If Jesus set them free from sin and spiritual death, wouldn't their inner natures strive for freedom in every area of their lives? After all, that's what happens when the Spirit is in control.

This renewal of 2025 has been occurring for several years now. New wineskins are required because the old, brittle ones can't cope with the new wine. Physical organizations and methodologies must be evaluated and changed to accommodate it. If those structures and their doctrinal slants do not allow for the new wine, the Holy Spirit will pass by them and go to those who do. From there the Spirit always flows outside sanctuary walls to be poured out on all flesh. As reformation removes spiritual waste, corruption, and unfruitfulness, the body of Christ becomes a more powerful and effective influence.

Most of us are aware of Martin Luther's Reformation, but other reformations have occurred since then, such as the twentieth century's Pentecostal Movement and Charismatic Renewal. I believe we have been in a new reformation since around 2016. Other credible prophets have offered various dates for its start ranging between 2012 and 2020. Regardless of when it began, we all agree that the church is in a new era.

Alongside this new move of the Spirit is a drastic increase in attacks against Christianity and a public, media-driven, militant vocalization of atheism, agnosticism, Marxism, militant Islam, witchcraft, and sorcery, as well as new age practices and nature worship. Only a Spirit-filled church operating in third-heaven authority can slay this newly risen demonic dragon.

One of the elements of the new Christian era is the Lion's army, which carries the fire of the Spirit. I live in Nevada, a state whose motto is Battle Born because it attained statehood during the Civil War. The Lion's army is likewise battle born but of the Spirit of God. Its warriors are believers who have risen up in this era to take on war mantles and creative anointings. This kind of warring involves binding, loosing, and (with spiritual authority) resisting what the devil is doing on earth. In addition, Jesus uses the Lion's army to release His plans and purposes. In other words, He uses our faith and authority to bring about His will "on earth as it is in heaven" (Matt. 6:10).

THE FIVE GRACES

One day while I was in prayer, the Lord revealed five areas of His church that are being reformed in this new Christian era. There are more, but these five help us understand what the Spirit is doing. Remember, the era's purpose is to increase the church's influence on the world. Jesus works through His people, the church. He changes us, and then we change the world.

Five is the number of grace, and these five areas are graces that are being released onto the earth—effects from the anointing of the Holy Spirit's presence coming upon us. They cannot be attained through our physical works; we must contend for them spiritually. That takes a willingness to step outside religion's status quo and become eager vessels through which He can flow.

Past reformations were Spirit breathed, and so is this one. But it's a new day, and the Spirit is breathing something fresh and alive for this era. So let's look into the five graces that are being released.

1. Worship

I was born and raised during a time when Christians talked and sang *about* Jesus. When the Charismatic Renewal came, believers began talking and singing *to* Jesus. In this new Christian era we are to worship *in the presence of* Jesus. The Holy Spirit is so strongly manifesting the presence of Jesus among us that worship is a matter of being with Him. The anointing is a piece of heaven in our midst, as we become enraptured. Jesus Himself is involved in the experience, and the divine intimacy experienced through this worship heals hearts and manifests miracles.

2. Word

We all need to know the Word of God. An intellectual understanding of the Word is one thing, but being transformed as the Holy Spirit gives divine revelations of the Word is another. The difference between the two experiences is great. A person can intellectually know the Word and not know the author. Yet when the Holy Spirit is in us, the Word becomes alive and has prophetic spontaneity. The Spirit speaks to us through the Word, illuminating our minds with understanding, wisdom, prophetic guidance, and motivation for our specific situations.

Jesus is the Word. "In the beginning was the Word, and the Word was with God, and the Word was God.... And the Word became flesh and dwelt among us, and we beheld His glory, the glory as of the only begotten of the Father, full of grace and truth" (John 1:1, 14). The Spirit of Jesus mentioned in Philippians 1:19 and Acts 16:7 is the

Holy Spirit. With the Holy Spirit of Jesus in us we become people of His living Word.

3. Warfare

This kind of spiritual warfare is waged with faith and authority as we look down from heaven's perspective, rather than looking up from an earthbound view. Only the Spirit can enable us to view things from this higher vantage point. In 2010 the Lord commissioned me with the assignment to teach His people how to walk in third-heaven authority. Third-heaven authority is a principle of the new era.

James said that we must be doers, not just hearers, of the Word (Jas. 1:22). That's a biblical imperative. Being a doer of the Word is a powerful act of spiritual warfare, but one problem can arise: If you don't have revelation of the Word, you will find yourself doing religion. The result is frustration that creates doubt and unbelief and that empowers the flesh. Spirit revelation empowers the heart to act with spiritual authority and faith.

4. Wonders

During this time, signs, wonders, miracles, and gifts of the Spirit are manifesting regularly, to the point of being expected. Jesus is displaying His great love for His people and using them to impact societies and nations. Many public signs and wonders will appear. This is how God intended it to be.

5. Winning

During this era the Holy Spirit is equipping believers to be winners. First, we'll have increased power to win the personal battles in our lives because we are walking in step with the Spirit. Second, there will be an anointing from the Spirit for mass evangelism to win souls to Jesus. Third, a spiritual awakening will be poured out on cultures and nations, winning them to God and bringing transformation. Reformation is taking place. The Lion's army is rising up. A new Christian era is here.

RENEW YOUR MIND TO THE NEW ERA'S PROPHETIC POSSIBILITIES

One day in my prayer time, the Holy Spirit spoke to me and said, "Renew your mind to the prophetic possibilities of this new era." This was not just for me but for the Lion's army, so let me repeat what the Spirit said: Renew your mind to the prophetic possibilities of this new era. By *prophetic possibilities* I sensed the Spirit referring to all things supernatural and to how walking in the Spirit opens the doors of our futures.

Paul wrote to the Roman church, *"Do not be conformed to this world*, but be transformed by the renewing of your mind, that you may prove what is that good and acceptable and perfect will of God" (Rom. 12:2). Paul was saying that being born again should change our ways of thinking. Instead of thinking as the world does and being driven by flesh, sin, selfishness, manipulation, and other aspects of the natural man, we should bring our minds into alignment with our new natures.

This doesn't just happen, however. Inside us a battle is raging between our old and new natures, between the world's way and God's way. We must "fight the good fight of faith, [and] lay hold on eternal life" (1 Tim. 6:12). Part of that fight involves becoming spiritually minded, which requires renewing our minds to the things that are in Christ Jesus so that we can think the way He thinks.

The word translated "conformed" in Romans 12:2 is from the Greek root word *schema*, which describes a pressure that's applied to conform something that's put into a mold. When this happens, the object being conformed ends up as a replica of the mold.[1] Paul was saying, "Don't allow the world to press you into its mold. That was your past, when you lived by the dictates of your old nature. Now you're saved. So get rid of the old way of thinking and be transformed."

The Greek term translated "transformed" is *metamorphoo*, from which we get the English word *metamorphosis*.[2] Physiologically, metamorphosis takes place when a caterpillar sheds its skin and becomes a butterfly. In Jesus Christ a spiritual metamorphosis takes place in us, and we become butterflies, so to speak. We become different; we are in the world but not of the world (John 17:16; 15:19).

The genetic composition of the lives within us will ultimately produce their end results. Once our thinking is released into the understanding of (1) who we are, (2) the beauty of our creation, and (3) our abilities to fulfill and to walk out all our natures in Christ Jesus, we no longer have to be conformed to the world and its ways of thinking. So don't let the world press you into its mold. Be transformed by the renewing of your mind and your thinking, and the renewing of how you approach things. It's interesting that being conformed is *natural* and takes no effort. Conformity just happens when we do nothing. However, being transformed is *supernatural*. God promises when we renew our minds to truth, He will transform us.

Let's take this charge to renew our minds a step further by including prophetic possibilities. When the Holy Spirit spoke to me and said, "Renew your mind to the prophetic possibilities of this new era," He was telling me to change my thinking to incorporate the idea that in the future God would have something better for me than what I'd experienced up to that point. He was saying, "Open your mind to the possibilities."

The way we have done church and conducted our Christian lives is changing. We must have a new mindset in order to receive the change and walk in it. This change does not in any way minimize our past experiences and revelations in Christ. Actually, it validates them. It means, however, that we are still too dependent on the natural man, the world's ways, and the world's systems, because they have infiltrated the body of Christ. In this new Christian era we must let go of the old ways and open ourselves to the possibilities the Holy Spirit opens to us.

Those possibilities are often prophetic in form because the Holy Spirit is inside us, the church of the Lord Jesus Christ. He is trying to show us an expanded, more glorious future. What the Spirit has done through the church throughout history has been good and pure and wonderful. He's used the body of Christ to profoundly touch the world. Yet there is more. The Holy Spirit is ramping things up to accomplish a greater work in these critical last days, and we must adapt to a new wineskin.

Part of adapting is reevaluating our spiritual habits and opening our spiritual eyes to prophetically see what Jesus wants His church to accomplish on the earth today. We cannot walk fully in obedience and embrace the new without changing some of our previous mindsets. One translation of Romans 8:5 says, "Those who live as their human nature tells them to, have their minds controlled by what human nature wants. Those who live as the Spirit tells them to, have their minds controlled by what the Spirit wants" (GNT).

The moment we hold on to the traditions of old purely because they make us feel comfortable and safe is the moment they become fleshly and religious works. Again, please understand what I'm *not* saying—I'm not saying we need to compromise or change biblical truth and foundational teaching. Rather, I am saying the Holy Spirit is calling us to step out into new applications of that truth. The Bible explains that God is changing us "precept upon precept, line upon line...here a little, there a little" (Isa. 28:10, MEV). It's about adding to and not removing or replacing the former. As God adds something, anything of the former that needs to be changed will be changed and then incorporated into the new, bringing a fresh breath and life. This is how the Holy Spirit keeps the church vibrant and alive. To keep from becoming dry and stale, we maintain what is good and remember that salvation and the life principles of the Spirit, the Holy Spirit's indwelling, and the laws of the Spirit are unchanging. He's altering the ways we allow the Holy Spirit to be manifested through us. Then we must yield to the Spirit and set our minds on Him rather than cling to everything from the past.

It's important to note that all this must be seasoned with God's grace. Blanket statements won't do. I am not saying that holding on to anything from the past automatically means that you've missed God or are in sin and that—*boom*—you're left behind while the others go on with Jesus. No, no, no. That's not grace. That's not what

I'm talking about. There is rest in Christ. We must learn to run our races at the pace of grace.

If we hold on to elements of the old that need to be changed, they will hinder us. One thing we absolutely can't hold on to is error. A huge error that has snaked its way into the body of Christ is the belief that we cannot know and understand the mind of God, especially in a practical sense for daily direction. That idea is not biblical. Listen to this: "But as it is written: 'Eye has not seen, nor ear heard, nor have entered into the heart of man the things which God has prepared for those who love Him.' *But God has revealed them to us through His Spirit.* For the Spirit searches all things, yes, the deep things of God" (1 Cor. 2:9–10).

It's through the Spirit that God's thoughts are revealed. A few verses later Paul wrote, "For 'who has known the mind of the LORD that he may instruct Him?' But we have the mind of Christ" (1 Cor. 2:16). The mind of Christ is the Holy Spirit and includes the views, feelings, character, and will of the Lord Jesus Christ. These things are revealed to us through His Word as the Holy Spirit illuminates our minds. The Holy Spirit also supernaturally reveals these things as He impresses them upon our minds. This in turn aligns our minds with Christ's thinking.

When Paul urges us to renew our minds, we do it according to God's Word, the Holy Spirit's direction, and His prophetic revelation. You have the choice and ability to renew your mind to the mind of Christ. When you do it, God promises to transform you. When you allow the metamorphosis to happen, the Holy Spirit overcomes your worldly thinking.

When we renew our minds, we surrender to the Spirit's revelatory abilities, the communication system of heaven.

Through the grid of Scripture, the Holy Spirit deposits into us the application, wisdom, and leadership we need to be transformed and to comprehend the mindset of Christ for this next era. We must go into the new season with a new mindset. Not everything from the old will be erased—only what the Holy Spirit wants us to discard in order to be ready for our future.

Seven Dynamics of Prophetic Possibilities

Following are seven dynamics, or principles, involved in renewing our minds to the prophetic possibilities of this new era. Some of the terminology may be familiar and may suggest old interpretations. Let the Spirit of God speak to you about that; allow Him to expand your definitions of certain words and phrases.

1. We must be God-inside minded.

God lives within us, not out there somewhere. "Do you not know," the Bible asks, "that your body is the temple of the Holy Spirit who is in you?" (1 Cor. 6:19). Grasp that truth. Believe it. Receive it. God, the Holy Spirit living inside us, has written His Word upon our hearts and regenerated our spirits. It's not about bombarding heaven as if we're trying to touch God out in the cosmos so He'll notice and answer our prayers. No. He's inside us via the Holy Spirit. He goes everywhere with us. He empowers us and gives us wisdom for all things. The body of Christ in this new Christian era must be God-inside minded.

2. We must be new-creation minded.

When Jesus came out of the tomb on the third day and then ascended to heaven, He became the firstborn of many brethren who would become new creations. The moment we accept Jesus as Savior, His Spirit (the Holy Spirit) comes into us, and we are born again, spiritually made like the firstborn, Jesus. He did not remake or renovate us; He made us completely and wholly new. Paul said, "If anyone is in Christ, he is a new creation; old things have passed away; behold, all things have become new" (2 Cor. 5:17). Being in Christ does not mean reverting to the image of the first Adam but means being in the image of the last Adam, the Lord Jesus Christ Himself. "So it is written, 'The first man Adam became a living being.' The last Adam became a life-giving spirit" (1 Cor. 15:45).

This is your new identity. We renew our minds to align with who we are and who's inside us. Then corresponding actions will follow as we walk in the Spirit in all things.

3. We must be righteousness minded.

Righteousness is not about being perfect in the flesh but is about recognizing our legal positions of righteous justification based on what Jesus accomplished on the cross. "For He made Him who knew no sin to be sin for us, that we might become the righteousness of God in Him" (2 Cor. 5:21). Once God's Spirit is in us, we are positionally justified, made perfectly righteous in our new natures. The Holy Spirit then begins the process of sanctifying us or conforming us to the image of Christ. For the believer it is a lifetime process of growing. "For by one offering [on the cross] He [Jesus] has perfected forever those who are being sanctified" (Heb. 10:14). We *are* perfected, and we are *being* sanctified.

That is the Holy Spirit's work in us, as we follow His lead. "If [we] are led by the Spirit, [we] are not under the law" (Gal. 5:18). In other words, it's no longer about trying to follow religious laws and rituals; it's about moving with the flow of the Spirit. He will never lead us into sin and bondage, but He will lead us into freedom and His purposes. As new creations in right relationship with the Lord, we are not trying to overcome, beat up, and control the flesh in order to experience this new Christian era. Because we are in right standing with Him, the power to walk in our righteous capacities in this natural realm comes from within and not from without.

Paul wrote about the futility of trying to control the flesh by the flesh. Summing it up, he said, "I say then: Walk in the Spirit, and you shall not fulfill the lust of the flesh" (Gal. 5:16). Absent the Spirit's influence our flesh can adopt animalistic ways. If we try to become righteous through behavioral modifications and energies of the natural realm, we will end up devouring ourselves. No! We must understand our identities in Christ and be righteousness minded.

4. We must be Word-of-God minded.

Before the Hebrews made it to the Promised Land, they had to become people of the Law. Being renewed in our new era requires that we are people of the New Testament. Paul wrote, "Be diligent to present yourself approved to God, a worker who does not need to be ashamed, rightly dividing the word of truth" (2 Tim. 2:15).

As I mentioned earlier, the Word of God is the grid through which the Spirit transforms us. But the Word is more than that. It is revelation; it is how God has chosen to reveal Himself so that His Spirit can bring life to us.

5. We must be warrior minded.

We are warriors. Yes, we are members of the body of Christ. Yes, we are living stones in the temple of God (1 Pet. 2:4–5). Yes, we are members of His family. The Bible offers various analogies to explain the dynamics of who we are in the Spirit and in our relationships with God. But we are also the army of God. Scripture tells us, "You therefore must endure hardship as a good soldier of Jesus Christ. No one engaged in warfare entangles himself with the affairs of this life, that he may please him who enlisted him as a soldier" (2 Tim. 2:3–4).

Being good soldiers engaged in this warfare demands being warrior minded, because in this day, we have to take things by force. "The kingdom of heaven suffers violence, and the violent take it by force" (Matt. 11:12). This scripture refers to the time of John the Baptist and Jesus. Life was going along as it had been for centuries when things suddenly opened up, and people's minds and hearts turned to the coming Christ. "What do we have to do?" they wondered. The answer: "We've got to take this thing by force."

So they rushed to John the Baptist and were baptized in water. Then Jesus stepped on the scene, and contrary to all the pressures from the world and even Judaism, they had to choose to believe and accept Him. They did this knowing they could be ostracized and disowned by their Jewish families. Many suffered persecution and even lost their lives. The situation was clear—they had to take things by force.

This new Christian era will also be taken by force. The overall structure of grace is here. Therefore, the force we exercise is our yielding to grace and what it offers us— empowerment to stand against the evil in the land, to take the kingdom, and to usher it in. With everything that's happening and trying to conform us—social ills, strife, political unrest, overt wickedness, good being called evil, evil being called good, sickness, and even global pandemics—we must *forcefully* push through, renewing our minds and being transformed by the Holy Spirit's power. This is the process of entering in, and it requires you to have the mindset of a warrior.

6. We must be evangelism minded.

We must always remember that our priority is leading others to Jesus while letting His life shine through us to the world. We are to "always be ready to give a defense to everyone who asks...a reason for the hope that is in [us]" (1 Pet. 3:15). Though the bulk of our ministry teaches on the prophetic and moving in it, CK and I are careful to never forget that soul winning is at the heart of all we do. God's desire is to see all men saved, and He chose us to be among His hands and feet.

The ultimate purpose for the prophetic and for warring in the Lion's army is to win souls from the enemy's grasp. The way you change a culture is by changing the hearts of men and women, one at a time. Look at how a handful of disciples turned the world upside down with a life-changing message! We must be evangelism minded, realizing that the release of God's power and the reality of what is happening are leading us into the new Christian era and the saving of souls. The ultimate purpose is for others to go to heaven with us.

7. We must be spiritually open-minded.

Being spiritually open-minded is not to be confused with being mindful in the world's way. My mentor Dave

Roberson used to say, "You can be so open-minded that your brain falls out onto the floor." This is what we are seeing today in the name of so-called tolerance. The world has become so open-minded that overt perversion and just plain insanity are accepted as normal.

On the other hand, being spiritually open-minded means seeing what the Lord is revealing through the Holy Spirit and being willing to embrace it as we enter this new era. Older Christians often get so locked onto the methodologies, frameworks, and experiences of the past that they become skeptics and close their minds to the new things that the Spirit has for us.

Again, talking about walking in the Spirit, in Galatians 5:25 Paul said, "If we live in the Spirit, let us also walk in the Spirit," or, as the NIV says, "Let us keep in step with the Spirit." Paul was speaking in military terms, regarding soldiers in formation. We walk, step by step, in line with the Holy Spirit. If He goes left, we go left. If He takes big steps, we take big steps. When He takes small steps, we take small steps too. When He confronts the enemy, we do the same, with Him. If He stops to get somebody saved in the grocery store, we flow right with Him. Being spiritually open-minded means walking in the Spirit in all things.

THE SPIRIT OF GOD IS BROODING OVER THE NEW ERA

A stirring is happening. Can you sense it? I can. Other spiritual leaders can too. The Holy Spirit is brooding over this new era. Things are being shifted into place as a fresh move and work of God are being birthed.

On the last Friday evening of 2023, CK and I were sitting on our living room couch watching videos of some dear minister-prophet friends. We were simply enjoying the videos when suddenly (as He's done so many times) the Holy Spirit overcame me and pulled me into the spiritual realm. I saw a swirling of rainbow colors, heard heavenly music, and felt a deep stirring of the Holy Spirit. He was moving, creating, overwhelming, overcoming, and overshadowing me. There are no adequate words to describe the experience. I turned to CK to tell her what was happening, and she said, "I can feel it. I can feel the Holy Spirit moving all around me." For the longest time the two of us just basked in the Holy Spirit's presence as He repeatedly washed over us.

"Lord, what's all this stirring about?" I asked.

He immediately answered, "I want you to read the beginning of Genesis."

So I opened my Bible to Genesis chapter 1. Then He said, "In this current place of darkness on the earth, My Spirit is brooding over My church and birthing a new work for this time."

I read, "In the beginning God created the heavens and the earth. Now the earth was formless and empty, darkness was over the surface of the deep, and the Spirit of God was *hovering over* the waters" (Gen. 1:1–2, NIV).

Here's how Strong's Definitions describes the Hebrew verb *rāḥap̄* (translated as "hovering" in the NIV): "to brood... [or] flutter, move, shake."[3] In the beginning the Holy Spirit hovered, brooded, fluttered, moved, and shook on the face of the deep. Why? Because He is the *Ruach*, the *Pneuma*.

Ruach is the Hebrew word for *spirit* that is used for the Holy Spirit, the Spirit of holiness.[4] *Pneuma* is the Greek

New Testament word for the same—the invisible yet real and powerful Spirit, who is spiritual essence, personality, and substance.[5] In Genesis 1:2 the Holy Spirit was upon the face of the waters in a spiritual cloud, or presence, brooding over the earth. The word *brood* means "to produce by or as if by incubation,"[6] much as a hen sits on her eggs until they hatch and then covers and protects her chicks.

While in this brooding state over the void and formless earth, God spoke, and the Spirit pulled together all the pieces to form creation. You know, the Holy Spirit has never left the face of the earth. He's still moving, rearranging, and shifting things while breathing new life into them according to the timing and purposes of God for each era.

Why did He draw me into the stirring of the Spirit on that night? Yes, He invited me to experience the way the Spirit was moving. Yet He also showed me something new that was coming. During our forty-six years of full-time ministry, CK and I have been fortunate to experience many wonderful encounters. However, I'd never had one such as this, where I was so absorbed, overcome, and overshadowed by the understanding that the Holy Spirit was doing something new.

It wasn't that the Spirit was coming again. He was already here. Nor was this something that had never happened before. It was a matter of what was needed—of what's necessary on our planet in this time frame. What's needed is for Him to release in a *new* way things that shake this planet. The shaking occurs not by simply coming upon the earth but by coming upon the people, beginning with the people of God.

The Holy Spirit is doing another creative work, and it's happening in our lifetimes. CK and I have enjoyed great moves of God's Spirit. We came in during the Charismatic Renewal and have seen great moves of God as they've come and gone. We've traveled to other cities to get in on revival and absorb the anointing. We crave it. Our hearts yearn for it because once you've been in the glory like that, you never want to leave it. Even though we have responsibilities to meet and decisions to make in our daily lives, the hunger within us keeps driving us toward our next chance to be with the Lord in that capacity.

This feeling is something similar to what CK and I feel toward each other. The Lord blessed me with a wife who is way above my pay grade. She's my lover, best friend, and life partner. When CK and I got married, we signed a contract. We have a legal form declaring our relationship, and we live our shared life on the basis of that. Still, we crave the time that we can spend together enjoying each other's presence and building our oneness.

With Jesus I'm just as saved as I ever was, but I crave the time to be with Him and make love with the Lord, if you will. There's something about spending time in the secret place—when the glory comes, nothing in this world can compare. I tried to write about that in my book *Third-Heaven Authority*, in the chapter dealing with the intimacy that we have with the Lord. We find two examples of this intimacy with scriptural kings—King David in the Old Testament and his intimacy with the Lord, and King Jesus in the New Testament and His intimacy with the Father. They understood that intimacy with the Lord was what sustained them and gave them life.

I've told CK many times that when we're together, when I hold her hand, when I hold her, or when I talk with her, I am strengthened. We are just as married as we are when we're apart, but the moments we have together strengthen me. Something happens on the inside. The same thing happens through my intimacy with God and the Holy Spirit. I absolutely crave when He comes and moves, and I feel it.

Yet I have the assurance that He never leaves me or forsakes me (Heb. 13:5). He's just as present when I don't feel Him as when I do, but the feeling of experiencing Him repeatedly comes upon me. There are instances of this in the Book of Acts, where it says that the Holy Spirit came, the people were filled with the Spirit, or the Spirit moved.

To some degree the body of Christ has been going through a dry spell for a couple of decades. But a fresh wind is blowing. Times of refreshment from the Holy Spirit are upon us. We've seen flashes of this popping up on campuses and in churches across the globe. We see a scriptural parallel in Exodus 40:34–35, where "the cloud covered the tabernacle of meeting, and the glory of the LORD filled the tabernacle. And Moses was not able to enter the tabernacle of meeting, because the cloud *rested above it*, and the glory of the LORD filled the tabernacle." Some versions say that the cloud "settled on" the tabernacle (v. 35, NIV, ESV, NASB). The Holy Spirit appeared in a cloud to hover, brood, shake, flutter, and move upon His people.

I love it when the power of God comes on someone, and they go down under the Spirit, especially when they have resisted and been skeptical about such things being possible. Then, *bam!* They're doing carpet time. I just love the manifestation. At times when I've experienced this, I've felt raw power in the Spirit's presence. It was life transforming and affected the way I moved forward. Yet the brooding I sensed in my encounter on the last Friday of

2023—the brooding happening over the earth for this new Christian era—seemed more power filled than those previous manifestations.

In Luke chapter 1 the angel appeared to Mary and talked to her about being impregnated by the Holy Spirit. We've read the story hundreds of times, but have we really? "The angel answered and said to her, 'The Holy Spirit will *come upon you*, and the power of the Highest will *overshadow you*'" (v. 35). The word translated "overshadow" in this case is not similar to casting a shadow upon something and creating shade. No, it's just the opposite. There's brilliance. In fact, Strong's Definitions says that the word *overshadow* here means "to envelop in a haze of brilliancy."[7] The Holy Spirit hovered and brooded over Mary, supernaturally impregnating her natural womb with the life of God. It was a creative miracle, as was what happened at the beginning of time.

On the Mount of Transfiguration, Jesus was with Peter, James, and John. "While [Peter] was still speaking, behold, a bright cloud overshadowed them" (Matt. 17:5). A bright cloud and brilliance overshadowed them, "and suddenly a voice came out of the cloud, saying, 'This is My beloved Son, in whom I am well pleased. Hear Him!'" (v. 5). Jesus was transfigured by the brightness of that glory. The Holy Spirit moved in a similar way in the moment of the immaculate conception—there was a haze of the brilliance of God's glory in the spiritual realm, and it manifested new life in the body of Christ and then the world.

I believe we will experience overshadowing individually and collectively in this new era. So be in position with a renewed mind, ready to receive new spiritual encounters in the Holy Spirit! I prophesy that the Spirit of God is brooding over the body of Christ and the world today. He is overshadowing and releasing a new manifestation of outpouring. I crave it and long for it. I'm looking forward to watching His brilliance break out around the world. Cities will be impacted, as will rural communities, campuses, and political arenas. Broken families will be restored. Physical healings will take place. There will be testimony after testimony of the Holy Spirit's power, and churches will explode with worship, spreading the spiritual fire. We will see street evangelism ministries as never before. Believers from every walk of life will be overshadowed by the Spirit of God and will no longer be afraid to stand up, even if it means being canceled, labeled as weird, or persecuted.

Yet I have to admit that I sometimes feel similar to Noah just preaching and preaching and preaching, and the Lord won't let me out of it. I keep preaching that we are on the cusp of the greatest revival, of a spiritual awakening that this planet has never seen, numerically speaking. I say *numerically* not because this revival is more important than previous ones. Nor will God's displayed power be greater than it was in any previous revivals. I am telling you that the effect of the revival here and now will be just as dynamic as any other time in history. But the world is more populated now, so the awakening will reach more people than any previous outpouring has.

Another exciting thing is that the Lord has told me to invite you to walk in what He is going to do. You are not required to do so, but if you would like to, the invitation is for you to open your heart to His moving and to receive the brooding of the Spirit of God, as He comes upon you.

You can participate in the creative aspect of what the Holy Spirit is doing in people.

The Lion's army will roar, but your roar is directly proportional to your participation in the Spirit's move. Accepting the invitation does not mean sitting back and intellectually or rationally saying, "Oh, that would be nice. I'd like to have that." No, you must open your heart, watch in anticipation, and receive. It is contending for the Spirit of God and for the ways that He touches and breathes His *Ruach* upon us. Accepting His invitation involves casting aside preconceptions and religious ideas that try to lock you in a framework of how the Holy Spirit is supposed to move. The Spirit of God will not be contained within religious rules, pride, or embarrassment, or anything else.

Therefore, we cast aside those restraints and say, "Come, Holy Spirit, and move upon me. Breathe new life into me. Catch me into the Spirit. Let me know You in the fullness and reality of what You are doing now. I will not be left out. I will not be left out. I will *not* be left out. Come upon me now. Come upon me *now*."

Speak those words to the Lord consistently, and I believe the Holy Spirit will answer and draw you in. Remember, however, that this is not about seeking an experience. It is about seeking more of Him. Part of your prayer could be, "More of You, Lord. More of You, Holy Spirit. I just want more of You."

I can assure you that I'm not perfect, and I have made my share of mistakes. It is only the ever-pouring, ever-faithful grace of God that sustains me and works through me. Anything that I have done right for God has been within the perspective of saying, "Lord, help me set my flesh aside, and I'll move in Your Spirit for Jesus Christ."

The stirring for this new Christian era is not about good feelings, chills, and goose bumps. The manifestations of God's Spirit will bring change and light into dark places. This world is hurting and lost. In many respects it is void and needs the creative ability of the Holy Spirit. But the Lord told me that it would happen in the church first. When I say *church*, I'm not talking about a building. It'll happen in the body of Christ, in those who receive the stirring and are swept into it as the Spirit comes upon them. They will be the ones manifesting the power of the Great Commission, going into all the world and preaching the gospel. They are those who are in the Lion's army.

Yes! They will perform miracles, signs, and wonders for God because when you are enraptured in the place of God, you cannot come out without something happening. Moses hid in the cleft of the rock. All he saw were the hind parts of God as He passed by, but the experience turned Moses' hair white, and his skin shone brightly. (See Exodus 33:20–23 and 34:29–35.) It changed him. It made him bolder, wiser, and more authoritative.

Let it do the same for you.

Chapter 10

SPIRIT-FILLED BELIEVERS MAKE THE BEST WARRIORS

ABOUT FOUR WEEKS after my first Lion's army vision, three angels walked into the room where I was teaching a class on third-heaven authority. Only their silhouettes and faint features were visible, but I had seen angels appear in that form before. I told the students, "I just saw three angels enter the room, and they are standing quietly at the back. It looks like they'll be part of the class tonight."

After teaching about the origin and flow of spiritual authority for about half an hour, I noticed a shift in the anointing in the room. I knew something was up, so I calmly announced, "It seems the angels have a message for us tonight, because I'm being drawn into the spirit realm and am starting to hear their words."

Everyone was quiet and tuned in to the Spirit as I listened. Then I repeated the angel's words out loud to the students. "Stand in authority for your country during these challenging times. The Lord has called the body of Christ in America to rise up in spiritual authority for this nation, then for Israel, and then for other nations."

The glory of the encounter overwhelmed me. A knowing, or understanding, was impressed upon me—when the founding fathers made a covenant with God for this nation, God foresaw that our trying times would come. He already knew we would be in a battle for the soul of America, which would be under siege by antichrist spirits. I could feel the strong delusions and mind-control tactics of what could only be described as forms of witchcraft and sorcery, and I sensed the Lord's anger toward them.

The encounter started to lift, and the angels vanished, so I asked the students to pray in tongues for a while. I felt the need to walk and pray for a bit, so I went out the front door of the building to walk on the sidewalk. When I stepped out the door, I was surprised to find the three angels standing there, waiting for me.

They said, "We have come from the council of Him who desires you to experience victory in the Spirit. Return and instruct your students to move beyond simply praying and asking God to change the United States. Encourage them to start decreeing over their nation what they believe in. You are teaching them about third-heaven authority. Now it's time to put that authority into action. There is a time to ask God to intervene, and there is a time to spiritually command what needs to be done. Decree things, and watch them come to pass. Remind the students that this perspective is not from man but from God. Tell them that warriors use authority to release spiritual energies as weapons of righteousness."

I immediately returned to class to share the messengers' words with the students.

THE SPIRIT-FILLED LIFE

One of the first keys to living a Spirit-filled life is to yearn for all that God has for you. While walking in love should always be your first and most important aim, Paul clearly urged believers to "eagerly desire gifts of the Spirit" (1 Cor. 14:1, NIV). Desiring these gifts is good, honorable, and biblical. It doesn't mean you are being self-centered or unbalanced, although the enemy would like you to think that. Being Spirit filled (a term coined by Charismatics and based on Ephesians 5:18) means simply allowing your life to be directed by the Lord Jesus Christ through the fullness of the Holy Spirit inside you. This includes the activation of spiritual gifts and, I'm going to boldly say, the baptism of the Holy Spirit with speaking in tongues. Regardless of the stigmas that the world and that religion may attach to these realities, they are critical to experiencing God's power and effectiveness.

That said, living a Spirit-filled life does not make one superior or somehow holier. Nor does it nullify the need for the work of grace. On the contrary, being Spirit filled should enhance grace. Any gift given by the Lord is given purely by grace and should lead to a spirit of humility. We allow ourselves to be filled to the point of overflowing with the Holy Spirit, and we accept all He offers so that we may be more effective in spiritual warfare. This equipping is by His power, not our own. It is why Spirit-filled believers make the best warriors.

Walking out life in step with the Spirit is an incredible journey of experiencing greater depths with God while engaging in the spiritual warfare to which He is calling us. This means attaining *all* the promises that God has given us, including His covenant blessings and provisions. It means that our prayers are hot and that we're walking in the spiritual realm just as instinctively as we walk in the natural realm, releasing spiritual power and God's glory into the earth. It means visions, dreams, and angelic encounters (like the one described at the beginning of this chapter), and it means navigating the heavens.

We will now explore some spiritual truths about what it's going to take for you, as a Spirit-filled believer, to occupy the land, whatever that land is for you—perhaps it is your personal intimacy with the Lord, or perhaps it is your family or your own spiritual gifts and anointing.

Fighting the Good Fight of Faith and Good Warfare

Paul told Timothy, his son in the Lord, to "fight the good fight of faith" (1 Tim. 6:12). In this warfare, before anything else, we are fighting "the good fight of faith." That fight, as I previously mentioned, is fought in the arenas of our minds. Remember, the mind is the hinge that allows the door to swing open and operate in both the spiritual and natural realms. The fight is a good fight for all the things God wants to happen in our lives.

Yet this fight extends far beyond our individual concerns and families; it reaches to your community, your nation, and the world. The world is changed by the people of God impacting their circles of influence, regardless of how small or large those circles may be. Their involvement produces ripple effects that extend their influences. For the past few years, and particularly as I write this in 2024, we have been engaged in a great fight for the soul of America. The three messenger angels that were sent to me affirmed this. The Lord wants to use us to impact this nation. We must allow ourselves to be vessels of His glory. Every believer is critical to the fight. It's a good fight because we're contending for what the Lord Jesus Christ has covenanted with our nation.

But how do we begin to fight the good fight of faith? Well, Romans 10:17 tells us. It says, "So then faith comes by hearing, and hearing by the word of God." The good fight of faith always begins with hearing the Word of God, which sparks faith in us. The Word of God "is alive and active" (Heb. 4:12, NIV), breathing divine expansion, revelation, and knowledge that help us conform to His will and purposes. Therefore, our foundation as Spirit-filled individuals must be the Word.

Earlier, in 1 Timothy, Paul wrote, "This charge I commit to you, son Timothy, according to the prophecies previously made concerning you, that by them you may wage the good warfare" (1:18). According to Paul, the way Timothy was to "wage the good warfare" was *by them*. The question is what *them* refers to, and the answer is *the prophecies*.

What an interesting scripture that is! Remember who was writing—it was Paul, who was Saul, a highly intelligent man who had earned the equal of a modern-day doctorate in Hebrew theology. He was a zealous, religious intellectual who was in training for the Sanhedrin Council and was on his way to Damascus with letters to persecute and arrest Christians. Then a bright light shone around him, knocking him to the ground and blinding him. Saul cried out, "Who are You, Lord?" (Acts 9:5; see also vv. 1–4).

A voice spoke out of the light, saying, "I am Jesus, whom you are persecuting. It is hard for you to kick against the goads" (v. 5).

Saul was converted through a *supernatural* experience. He then asked Jesus what He wanted him to do. It's interesting that Jesus didn't tell him directly but instructed Saul to go on to Damascus, where he would receive further instruction. So Saul's companions led him there, and he waited (vv. 6–9).

Meanwhile, the Lord gave a reluctant disciple named Ananias a vision and sent him to Saul with a message. Saul's eyes were supernaturally healed through Ananias' hands and mouth. Saul was also filled with the Holy Spirit, baptized, and given a divine assignment to the Gentiles (vv. 10–20). All this happened because God gave a vision to Ananias, a brother in the Lord, and he obeyed.

From then on Saul was led by the Spirit. He began using the name Paul, which was given to him as a Roman citizen. He was as highly intelligent and intellectual as ever, yet he had been transformed by the Spirit inside him. He learned to walk in the Spirit, and he experienced the supernatural, including seeing angels. One appeared to him and kept him and a shipload of other people from drowning (Acts 27:18–25). Paul even mentioned being caught up to the third heaven (2 Cor. 12:2).

Many supernatural things happened in Paul's life. So when he told Timothy to wage good warfare by prophecies, Timothy understood exactly what Paul meant. Notice when Paul spoke of *the prophecies*, he didn't mention the last sermon that you heard. Sermons are necessary and should be inspired by the Spirit, but the Spirit has more than sermons in His arsenal. It includes what the Amplified Bible, Classic Edition calls *prophetic intimations* in its translation of 1 Timothy 1:18, which says, "This charge and admonition I commit in trust to you, Timothy, my son, in accordance with *prophetic intimations* which I formerly received concerning you, so that inspired and aided by them you may wage the good warfare." *Prophetic intimations* are words given directly from the Holy Spirit. Another translation of the verse says, "Use *these prophecies* in faith and with a clear conscience to fight this noble war" (GW). Still another says, "Use *those words* as weapons in order to fight well" (GNT). *Those words* are supernaturally spoken prophecies.

The prophecies mentioned in 1 Timothy 1:18 are supernatural revelations from the Holy Spirit that do not originate in the intellects of men. They aren't from a man's charge or direction but are revelations from the Holy Spirit through spoken words. Those spoken words can come via another believer or from the Holy Spirit, straight to our spirits. Sometimes such words seem audible, and sometimes we have an internal knowledge of the information, understanding, detail, or guidance that comes to us. In each case, they are gifts of the Spirit. For some, they come via visions, dreams, and angelic visitations. Paul experienced all these inspirations. They were transformative and conveyed God's will. However, Paul also used them as weapons against the enemy to wage a good warfare. Now his words are giving us insight into how to do the same.

THE POWER OF GRACE

At one point in his life, Paul struggled with his notorious "thorn in the flesh" (2 Cor. 12:7). For centuries scholars have debated what the *thorn* was. Personally, I believe it was the intense persecution and spiritual attacks Paul was under. Regardless, he pleaded with the Lord three times that He would remove it (v. 8). After the third time, the Lord said, "My grace is sufficient" (v. 9).

You have to ask yourself, "Why did the Lord give Paul that answer?" It wasn't a random response to make him feel better—not at all. The Lord had a specific purpose in mind. He wasn't saying, "Just calm down, Paul, and go with the flow. Whatever happens happens. It'll be either good or bad, but know that I've got you." Those might be nice sentiments, and yes, we can rest in God's grace, but that's not what the Lord meant. I believe He was saying, "Paul, you've learned that in My grace I've given you everything you need to be victorious. Now use it. It's sufficient grace."

The Spirit's revelations to you are always under the realm of grace. His grace is sufficient and powerful. Paul learned how to use grace, revelation, and prophecy, as well as spiritual encounters, as what? As weapons! That's why Spirit-filled believers make the best warriors in the Lion's army!

For example, Paul used his supernatural encounter with Jesus as a defense and a weapon, testifying to it during his audience before King Agrippa. It was a physical defense to the king, a defense that also decreed the truth to the wicked spirits that were behind Paul's persecution. Paul said,

> As I journeyed to Damascus with authority and commission from the chief priests, at midday, O

king, along the road I saw a light from heaven, brighter than the sun, shining around me and those who journeyed with me. And when we all had fallen to the ground, I heard a voice speaking to me and saying in the Hebrew language, "Saul, Saul, why are you persecuting Me? It is hard for you to kick against the goads." So I said, "Who are You, Lord?" And He said, "I am Jesus, whom you are persecuting. But rise and stand on your feet; for I have appeared to you for this purpose, to make you a minister and a witness both of the things which you have seen and of the things which I will yet reveal to you. I will deliver you from the Jewish people, as well as from the Gentiles, to whom I now send you, to open their eyes, in order to turn them from darkness to light, and from the power of Satan to God, that they may receive forgiveness of sins and an inheritance among those who are sanctified by faith in Me."

—ACTS 26:12–18

Can you imagine standing before a king in his public court, and your defense is to tell him how Jesus appeared to you and told you to do the very thing for which you are now being prosecuted? In essence Paul said that his obedience to his encounter with Jesus was the way he was going to win the fight!

I had an encounter years ago in which the Lord Jesus took me to heaven to talk to me. While I was there, He showed me this massive, circular building with many, many rooms. I call it the "revelation building." It reminded me of the Pentagon in Washington, DC. Inside were multiple circular halls and straight halls that intersected across the diameter of the building.

Jesus said, "I want to teach you about revelation in the Spirit." Then He took me through the outside door to the first room and said, "The room that we're now entering is the salvation room. The way you get in to this building is salvation." As He opened the door and as we stepped into the room, He said, "Notice that as we go through the door, you are in a room. You are not in an intellectual concept or in understanding. Spiritual revelation occupies an area, and it's important to bring your own presence into that area. While you are there, you take ownership of the room by your faith. When you do this, you are able not only to stay and operate there but to use all that is available within the room. That's called *authority*, and revelation brings authority."

After that, Jesus took me to the other end of the room and opened a door that led to the halls and other rooms. Pointing down the hall, He said, "There's the baptism in the Holy Spirit room. There's the love room. There's the healing room." Each room was an area of revelation for specific purposes.

"In order for you to have all that I've given unto you," Jesus continued, "you have to go into the rooms, occupy them, and manifest your authority." Jesus' message was about prophetic revelation that the Holy Spirit manifests when He quickens and inspires us. And again, whether it is spoken or is a knowing in your spirit—whether it comes via visions, dreams, angels, the Word of God on a printed page, or the Holy Spirit speaking *rhema* words to you for personal direction—it is revelation. *Rhema* words from the Holy Spirit are every "utterance" and word spoken by

Him.[1] Regardless of how revelation comes, it has borders and an atmosphere.

In the Spirit, when I walked into the salvation room with the Lord, there were four walls that created the room's defining boundaries. The moment you enter a physical room, you know where its boundaries are because you see its walls. That is what God's truth (His Word) does in the spiritual realm—it defines the boundaries of spiritual revelation.

As you enter a physical room, you not only see its boundaries but also experience the room's atmosphere. In the spiritual realm the Spirit's grace and energies make up the atmosphere. You could refer to this as anointing. Revelation has borders and atmosphere in the Spirit. Let me just clarify what I'm not saying here: I'm not saying that there is a literal, permanent revelation building in heaven. I'm telling you that the Lord chose to reveal this truth to me through what He showed me. That is how it works in the spiritual realm.

If at first you don't understand all that, it's OK, as long as your faith foundation is firm in what Jesus did for you on the cross. When I was in my mother's womb, for example, I didn't know I was going to be born. And when I was born, I didn't have any part in making it happen. From my perspective it just happened. Later, however, I learned how it happened.

The same can be said of when I was born again—I didn't fully understand what transpired, but as I grew, I learned how it happened. That's my point. I'm saying that if you can be born again by simply trusting Jesus without understanding the dynamics and details of what's occurring, then you can operate in any revelation, any prophecy, any inspiration from the Lord, and any scripture that jumps off the page and slams you in the heart. By faith, you simply operate in those things. As you mature and learn how it works, you enter a different area of faith and power in God.

Prophetic revelation creates an atmosphere for presence, specifically God's presence, because God's the One who does it. He is one with His Spirit. God creates the atmosphere and invites us to join Him in it. Just as the Lord invited me to walk into the rooms with Him, I believe He's inviting you too.

Revelation operates by these principles and creates an atmosphere for presence to occupy. God will always occupy it and meet us there. When you bring your presence into prophetic revelation and join Him, the fusion of your faith with the revelation He spoke releases anointing and power. We accept what He reveals as truth, and the atmosphere of grace both makes it ours and gives us the authority to operate in it. We also invite others into the room when we share what God has done for us. That's why we give testimonies. That's why we share prophecies. And that's why I share the visions and encounters that I've had.

FULL CIRCLE

Coming full circle with all this, we see how prophetic revelation becomes a weapon to be used against the enemy's assaults. Of course, we pick up the sword of the Spirit and put on the armor of God by following the Word of God (Eph. 6:17, 11). That's never in question. Nevertheless, it is both the Word and the Spirit—both the Word and the atmosphere of power that flows within it.

In my sermons I often speak about spiritual streams of revelation. That's just another way of describing these principles. When the Holy Spirit reveals divine mysteries to us, He creates a spiritual stream of revelation that we can re-access later. Then, by our faith we can release the anointing that the stream contains.

Over time, however, it's common to forget something the Spirit showed you years or even weeks ago. But don't worry! Jesus said, "The Helper, the Holy Spirit, whom the Father will send in My name, He will teach you all things, and bring to your remembrance all things that I said to you" (John 14:26). Just as the Holy Spirit reminded the disciples of what Jesus had told them when He walked with them in the flesh, the Holy Spirit will bring to your remembrance the written Word and the prophetic words the Lord has spoken. When He does, you can access the same faith and anointing you had before, and you can use them as weapons against the enemy's tactics. It's like drawing spiritual weapons out of your spiritual holster.

But let's go one step further. When the Holy Spirit shows you things to come (meaning future events or wisdom that will be needed), those prophetic words form a spiritual memory of the future that can release the creative anointing of God into your life before the future event ever happens. By *creative* I mean that you become a co-laborer with the Spirit in making the words come to pass. You are a participant in releasing your own destiny.

That is why Paul instructed Timothy to take extra care in remembering the prophecies. Timothy had to revisit them in faith because by them he would wage good warfare and fight the good fight.

THE INVITATION

Jesus is giving out invitations to walk into the room with Him. Will you accept? While you're in the room with Jesus, you will find the following.

- **Purpose**: You now have an assignment and another invitation to partner with Him.

- **Direction**: You're motivated to focus your attention and spiritual energies on the assignment.

- **Faith**: You not only believe the Lord but actively engage your attitudes, words, and behaviors to align yourself with Him.

- **Authority**: You accept the responsibility to rise up in the Spirit and use your spiritual authority.

- **Power**: You watch miracles happen and use those encounters as weapons against the devil.

We must always use wisdom and discernment in understanding that prophetic revelation has spiritual dimensions and atmosphere. Just as you can't take the parables of Jesus out of context and apply what He taught to anything, prophetic revelations are for specific assignments with specific boundaries. The parables were limited to the revelations that Jesus was giving to the people. When He said that the kingdom of God is similar to a small mustard seed that when planted grows into a tree large enough to house the birds of the air (Mark 4:30–32), He was talking about the growing ability of that seed, the Word of God, and how it blesses and benefits us.

Remember, however, that the revelation within the parable has spiritual dimensions. You can't extrapolate from it to say, "OK, I'm going to start the First Church of the Mustard Seed, and in order to be saved, each member must carry a mustard seed in his or her pocket." If you say that, you would operate outside the dimension of the truth that Jesus' parable implied. When you do that, you go off into weirdness, with no grace and no power. But within the truth, you have the atmosphere of God (which includes His grace), and you know that He has invited you there with Him. Therefore, you can release everything that you need to operate in life and victory.

I daresay there have been times when the Lord has spoken to you personally and given you wonderful revelations, including prophecies about your own life, future, or destiny. Don't forget them. Keep them active by your faith. They are still working in the Spirit. Speak and pray the revelations that are in those rooms you've entered. And do what Paul told Timothy to do—purposefully use the revelations as weapons to wage a good warfare.

Chapter 11

GRACE IS THE ASSURANCE OF A PROPHETIC LIFE

ROM THE MOMENT CK and I received the baptism in the Holy Spirit, the supernatural realm opened, and we entered a truly miraculous, prophetic life. To this day learning the ways of the Spirit is an adventure. We are continually learning and always wanting more of what the Lord has.

During the first four years of our Spirit-filled lives, we launched out to do everything the Word of God told us we could do. If there was a scripture on it, we did it. We trained ourselves to pick up on the slightest spiritual impressions that we felt may possibly be the leading of the Spirit. We learned and grew through each situation. Along the journey we saw numerous people saved, baptized in the Spirit, healed, and delivered. Miracles occurred everywhere we went.

All those things were wonderful. However, the most important things to us were our relationships with the Holy Spirit Himself. During those years, we read loads of books and listened to hundreds of cassette tapes on the subjects of the Holy Spirit, faith, spiritual authority, and miracles. One day while reading about what Jesus went through in the hours between His death and resurrection, I had an encounter with God.

Overcome by the Holy Spirit, I began to shake and weep for the millions of people who had never heard the complete truth about Jesus' sufferings and resulting victory. Even if they'd heard enough to believe that He died and rose from the dead for the forgiveness of their sins, I realized that their shortened versions of the gospel overlooked the mysteries that unlock great revelation and power. It's similar to making a sandwich with two pieces of fresh bread but nothing in the middle.

Paul understood this when he wrote, "That I may know Him and the power of His resurrection, and the fellowship of His sufferings, being conformed to His death, if, by any means, I may attain to the resurrection from the dead" (Phil. 3:10–11). Paul was saved, but he wanted to know Jesus more and to know more of the power that came with that relationship.

The experience I had while reading that book affected me so profoundly that I couldn't keep from sharing it with CK that evening. I told her how the Spirit was also pulling me into full-time ministry and how I felt supernaturally compelled to preach the whole gospel message with intense power. As she listened to me pouring out my heart, an anointing filled the room. Then CK shared what the Spirit had been saying to her, and she added that she was all in.

With the Holy Spirit's confirmation, the two of us were in full agreement. When that happens, watch out! One person can really put a thousand to flight, but two can send ten thousand packing! (Deut. 32:30). Although we were a team in those early stages, we had no idea what our kind of ministry would even look like. I had some reservations, and so did CK. Both of us had experienced deep hurt from traditional churches that had been controlling and abusive at times and that were totally against how the Spirit was using us. Despite the pain and rejection, we recognized the leading of the Holy Spirit and were willing to trust and obey Jesus.

Many have asked us how we knew that it was Jesus, and not just our emotions and assumptions, calling us into full-time ministry. The simple answer is this: By that time, we had become familiar with the voice of the Lord, and His words left driving desires and passions within our hearts. Another important question involved how we could trust that we would be successful. While it definitely required a step of faith, it was not an unreasonable or foolish step. We could trust the Holy Spirit because of His faithfulness to us during those first four years. He backed up every word of knowledge, every word of wisdom, and every prophecy.

Even so, what assurance did we have that the Spirit would back up this prophetic revelation? I would say that a prophetic life is a supernatural life. I'm using the word *prophetic* here in a general way to cover all the miraculous aspects of God. If you are born again, the Holy Spirit speaks to you. It's that simple. I'm talking about the voice of God, dreams, visions, the gifts of the Holy Spirit, signs, wonders, and angelic visitations. I'm talking about healings and casting out demons, as well as everything that is born by the Holy Spirit moving upon and in you, bringing supernatural revelation, direction, and wisdom. All those things have a prophetic and miraculous nature to them.

The Holy Spirit oversees the communication system of heaven. He is the One who reveals and transmits all truth to us, including future truth. Scripture says, "When He, the Spirit of truth, has come, He will guide you into all truth; for He will not speak on His own authority, but whatever He hears He will speak; and He will tell you things to come" (John 16:13). That means everyone can hear the voice of God calling them to salvation, because the Holy Spirit brings it to them. The Spirit doesn't suddenly stop speaking when a person gets saved. Once He's inside you, you are His temple and He speaks even more. Why would the Holy Spirit be inside us and not speak? That would not make sense!

The Spirit also manages the power flow from heaven. Everyone who receives the Holy Spirit has the supernatural power of God available to them. Scripture says this plainly: "You shall receive power when the Holy Spirit has come upon you" (Acts 1:8). This is the prophetic nature of the church. It involves all the ways in which the Spirit communicates to us, plus all the ways the Spirit releases spiritual power into and through us. Although it's for everyone who has been born again, the majority of born-again people don't realize that. Therefore, they don't develop or walk in this power.

To me the prophetic lifestyle makes perfect sense. It's simply flowing with the Holy Spirit and allowing Him to energize us any way He chooses. In previous chapters I detailed the spiritual gifts and gave examples of how they manifest. Knowing these details is important, but it is more important to know the Holy Spirit personally and develop a primary dependence on His indwelling presence. We don't need to consciously think about which combination of energies, gifts, anointings, and supernatural manifestations is in operation in a given moment. We can just enjoy the flow of the Spirit.

Since that first night when CK and I were baptized in the Holy Spirit, we have grown enough to flow with the Spirit without having to analyze or think about it too much. The supernatural life has become our normal life together. When we first started out, we used to think about it. Now our focus is on the fullness of our relationships with the Spirit. It's similar to our marriage. We know each other so well that we flow through life harmoniously. There's an ease about being together and having the same goals, as well as deferring to one another's wisdom and abilities. For those who desire a supernatural life, staying close to the Holy Spirit builds their skill levels and credibility.

A Prophet's Perspective of Grace

Now let's look at the subject of grace from a slightly different perspective—that of a prophet. As a prophet I can write from this point of view. What I'm teaching has come from decades of studying God's Word and watching it play out through the numerous spiritual experiences I've had.

To become skilled in the ways of the Spirit, we must first learn an important principle: Grace is the assurance of our prophetic lives because grace is what makes prophetic revelation sure. In other words, to really put faith in what the Spirit is revealing, something must guarantee it. According to Paul, the assurance and guarantee of revelation is grace.

Let me explain this principle through an example, in the fourth chapter of Romans, of how it unfolded for Abraham.

> For what does the Scripture say? "Abraham believed God, and it was accounted to him for righteousness."... Therefore it is of faith that it might be according to grace, so that the promise might be sure to all the seed, not only to those who are of the law, but also to those who are of the faith of Abraham, who is the father of us all.
>
> —ROMANS 4:3, 16

Remember my working definition of *grace*? It is the unmerited favor and empowering presence of God enabling us to (1) be who He created us to be, and (2) do what He has called us to do. Grace is like an umbrella covering our redemption and lives in Jesus. As we learned earlier, however, grace also enables and empowers our unique spiritual giftings, along with everything the Spirit shows and tells us prophetically.

Think about it. Abraham lived in the pagan city of Ur. His father and everyone around him worshipped idols. It is likely that Abraham did too. There was no Israel, no Torah, no Law, no Isaac, no Jacob, no Moses, no David, and no prophets. None of them had yet entered the scene. But the Lord showed up out of the blue one day to talk to Abraham and tell him he was chosen. Then God gave Abraham specific instructions that disrupted the course of his life.

The whole encounter was supernatural and prophetic. Even so, it took faith on Abraham's part to accept that what he heard was God's voice. He needed faith to align his life with the words God spoke to him. Yet the Bible calls God's prophecy to Abraham a promise. A biblical promise is a freely given pledge on the basis of God's will. The words God spoke to Abraham not only inspired faith but created an atmosphere within the promise that filled it with grace and power.

Prophetic grace is the atmosphere, and it becomes the assurance that what is revealed will come to pass. Consider Romans 4:16 in the Amplified Bible, Classic Edition: "Therefore, [inheriting] the promise is the outcome of faith and depends [entirely] on faith, in order that it might be given as an act of grace (unmerited favor), to make it stable and valid and guaranteed to all his descendants." Grace is what makes every promise from God sure, *stable*, *valid*, and *guaranteed*.

"But don't we have to obey?" you may ask.

Of course! That's what faith is about. Yet faith can believe and trust only in what grace has already given as a sure offer—a stable, valid, guaranteed offer. Our faith then is the assurance of receiving the manifestation, because grace is already the assurance that God has given us His promise.

That is basically what Paul was saying in Romans 5:1–2. "Therefore, having been justified by faith, we have peace with God through our Lord Jesus Christ, through whom also we have *access* by faith into this grace in which we stand, and rejoice in hope of the glory of God."

Notice the word *access*! The Amplified Bible, Classic Edition says we have "access (entrance, introduction)" (v. 2). You enter into grace by your faith, and your faith is a response to grace. The promise is prophetic truth, which contains an atmosphere of grace. The Amplified Bible, Classic Edition also speaks of us standing "firmly and safely" in God's grace (v. 2). That's security. Nothing can forcibly remove us from God's grace. The devil can't do it. Our friends can't do it. Neither our families nor our enemies can do it. Not even our circumstances can remove us from God's grace.

However, confusion, ignorance, shame, condemnation, doubt, and unbelief can affect our faith and cause us to lose sight of grace. The good news is that God's grace never leaves us. Spurgeon said it well: "The rain of his grace is always dropping; the river of his bounty is ever-flowing, and the well-spring of his love is constantly over-flowing."[1] You can get right back on your faith and pick up where you left off. This applies to all revelations that are given to you throughout your life—everything from your salvation to the Holy Spirit personally leading you in the flow of spiritual gifts.

Remember the encounter I described in the previous chapter about when Jesus showed me the revelation building? When I went into the first room, the salvation room, there were walls, a floor, and a ceiling, meaning the revelation had defined parameters. There was also an atmosphere within the room and a door that provided access. The walls, floor, and ceiling represent revelation. The atmosphere of the room represents the Spirit of grace, and the door represents faith, by which we gain access to the room.

"For the law was given through Moses," wrote John, "but grace and truth came through Jesus Christ" (John 1:17). Grace and truth are companions. The Bible is absolute truth. We know that. But let's frame it a little differently so we can grasp the prophetic aspect of truth. When God spoke to Abraham by revelation, Abraham didn't have scriptures for it. But God's promise matched what would eventually become Scripture. More than four hundred years later Moses wrote the Pentateuch, which became part of God's written Word and covered Abraham's experience. All revelations that come from the Father, from Jesus, and from the Holy Spirit are forms of spiritual truth. The following illustration helps us get a clearer picture.

Grace and Truth

Grace and Truth Come Through Jesus Christ
(John 1:17)

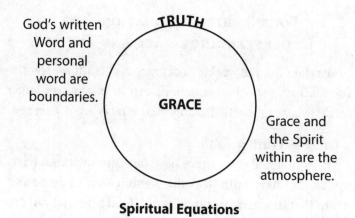

God's written Word and personal word are boundaries.

TRUTH

GRACE

Grace and the Spirit within are the atmosphere.

Spiritual Equations

- Grace + Truth = Faith
- Grace + Truth + Time = Success
- Grace – Truth = Confusion, Subjectivity, and Presumption
- Truth – Grace = Legalism and Lifeless Works

God's written Word and personal word are boundaries of spiritual revelation, as represented by the circle in the illustration. The Bible, the written Word of God, is the *logos* of God,[2] and every word spoken to us by the Spirit is the *rhema* (or *rēma*) of God.[3] Both contain the promises of God. The revelation sets the spiritual boundaries of what we can believe or expect from God.

In the illustration grace and the Spirit within the circle compose the atmosphere of a revelation. Grace is always given with the promise to make the revelation sure so our faith can then access it. God would never reveal something to you apart from His accompanying grace. If He did, your intellect and flesh would have to (or would try to) produce the revelation's fulfillment. The atmosphere of grace empowers you to walk out the revelation, and your faith gives you access.

FOUR SPIRITUAL EQUATIONS FOR UNDERSTANDING GRACE AND TRUTH

Understanding the workings of grace and truth is essential. The following spiritual equations can help us grasp larger truths where grace, truth, and their effects are concerned.

1. Grace + Truth = Faith

Without grace you cannot have faith, and without truth you cannot have faith. It is the combination of grace and truth that triggers spiritual faith. God's revelation creates the room, and the Spirit's grace fills the atmosphere, allowing your faith to get you through the door.

2. Grace + Truth + Time = Success

Even though time is in our natural realm, God relates to us here. There is a divine timing involved with the fulfillment of His promises. Unless we realize this, we will become discouraged when the promise seems delayed and faith wanes. By faith and patience we inherit His promises (Heb. 6:12).

3. Grace – Truth = Confusion, Subjectivity, and Presumption

How can you have grace where there is no promise based in truth? If you don't really believe (or you believe only part of) a promise that's given, you become wishy-washy, confused, and presumptuous. But presumption is not faith. Neither is the need to see how things work out before you believe. Grace does not fill what-ifs and maybes. It fills truth.

4. Truth – Grace = Legalism and Lifeless Works

Technically, this equation refers to assumed truth. With grace missing, assumed truth can produce only legalistic performances and lifeless works driven by a sense of obligation rather than true inspiration.

Grace Gems

Over the years, I've learned some interesting concepts about God's grace. I call them grace gems. They are precious truths that help keep me planted firmly in the ways of the Spirit. Here are just a few of them:

- Grace springs from God's responsibility toward us, while faith springs from our responsibilities toward Him.

- Grace causes God to initiate toward us, while faith causes us to respond to Him.

- Grace contains God's promises, and faith accepts those promises.

- Grace relates to who we are in Christ and to His promises to us, while faith relates to what we do about them.

- Grace is when God's hand reaches down. Faith is when our hands reach up. When the two connect, miracles happen.

- Grace requires faith; legalism requires fleshly performance.

- Grace is the relational structure of heaven; legalism is the relational structure of hell.

- When we change kingdoms, from darkness to light, God expects us to also change systems—from legalism to grace.

- Bringing legalism into God's kingdom results in religious works of performance, or legalism wrapped in religious garb.

- Religious works are the flesh's ways of trying to understand and serve God without revelation from the Spirit.

- Religious works attempt to force God into doing things one way rather than prompt us to conform to His way.

- Grace is the result of the blood sacrifice of Jesus, whereas legalism attempts to work around it.

MISCONCEPTIONS ABOUT GRACE

Among Christians there are many misconceptions about grace. Let's address some of them, and then I'll point out what God's Word says is true.

Misconception 1: Grace kicks in when you don't have enough faith to get the job done.

Have you ever thought that? Or do you know someone who has? They may have said something such as, "I'm having trouble believing for that, so I'm just going to throw myself on the grace of God." They confused grace with mercy. Grace is God's attitude toward the undeserving; mercy is His attitude toward those who err. You can throw yourself on God's mercy when you ask for forgiveness of sin, but it is faith (and not its lack) that keeps you in His grace.

Truth: Faith is a response to grace. You can't have faith without it (Rom. 4:13; Eph. 2:8).

Misconception 2: We access grace only after we have done everything we can by our own abilities.

Grace authorizes and empowers everything we do in God's kingdom. If our services as believers are lacking grace, then they are nothing more than fleshly works. Here's the difference: When we are Spirit led and moving in grace, the Spirit empowers all that we do.

Truth: If your efforts are not born of grace, they cannot be credited to you as righteousness (Rom. 4:1–5; Gal. 3:1–3).

Misconception 3: Grace allows us to sin.

My point here is not *if we sin*. We *do* sin. My concern is the erroneous belief that grace makes sin OK. Repentance corrects sin and releases God's forgiveness (1 John 1:9). However, as I mentioned, God's mercy heals the breaches in our relationships with Him. The attitude that sinning doesn't matter because God's grace covers it is in error.

Truth: The power of sin is flesh and legalism. Righteousness is empowered by grace (Rom. 6:11–15).

Misconception 4: Grace means we don't have to obey God or be responsible for our actions. It's a get-out-of-jail-free card.

Personal responsibility and obedience are big things with God. To judge your motives, He looks at your heart, not the weakness of your flesh. It's your individual responsibility to be Spirit led, to walk righteously, and to be accountable to Jesus (Gal. 5:25).

Truth: Grace produces the highest kind of responsibility, because it requires that you direct all the energies and efforts from your heart toward fulfilling God's will (1 Cor. 15:9–10).

Misconception 5: Grace leads to disorganization and chaos, and anything goes.

Chaos and confusion have nothing to do with grace. Grace is a principle that helps God's highly organized kingdom run smoothly and effectively. Going back to the revelation building analogy, grace is the atmosphere of a room with well-defined boundaries.

Truth: Grace represents the unshakable order of God's kingdom (Heb. 12:25–29).

Misconception 6: Grace is weak and passive.

There's a tendency for us to rationalize bypassing the Spirit and going straight to our own strengths and abilities to get the job done *for* God rather than *with* God. When Abraham and Sarah did that, they created Ishmael, a son of the flesh. Isaac was the son of promise, born of grace. When we attempt to make God's promises happen by our own means, we birth Ishmaels (Gal. 4:23). I think Paul had this in mind when he said, "I do not set aside and invalidate and frustrate and nullify the grace (unmerited favor) of God" (Gal. 2:21, AMPC).

Truth: In Scripture grace is never confused with passivity or failure. It's always coupled with truth, confidence, and power (John 1:14; Acts 4:33; Heb. 4:12).

In the next chapter we'll look at the importance of a robust faith. But before we do, let's remember that we are focused on the ways of the Spirit. The better we understand the Holy Spirit's ways of interacting with us, the more skilled we can become at walking in His ways.

Chapter 12

FAITH IS THE
SUBSTANCE OF A
PROPHETIC LIFE

WHETHER I'M READING a book or watching a movie, I love a good story. Some stories have not only entertained and inspired me but also motivated me to adjust my lifestyle. However, unless the Holy Spirit illuminates something in those stories and reveals a hidden spiritual truth, none of them produce spiritual faith in me. Yet even when the Spirit does that, it is only His revelation that sparks spiritual faith, not the story itself.

When the Holy Spirit drew me into the other realm and I watched the Lion's army visions play out, they released a supernatural faith deep within me. It was the kind of faith that causes men and women of God to reach beyond their natural abilities and do miraculous things by the authority of Jesus.

One of the ways of the Spirit is the way of faith.

Almost daily I launch my warfare while looking down from heaven's perspective, rather than looking up toward heaven from earth. I take authority over and pray against the demonic shriekers and screamers, the punishers, the enforcers, and the lying unity. When I do, I have no doubt in my heart that the warfare is effective, and I am confident that I hit my targets.

Every prophetic revelation that I've ever experienced—every *rhema* scripture and every word from the Holy Spirit, as well as every vision, dream, word of knowledge, or word of wisdom—has invited me to believe from my inner man. Spiritual faith is believing with our hearts to the point that we are willing to act in the physical realm.

Earlier I shared the story of how, in obedience to the Lord, CK and I moved our ministry from Oregon to Las Vegas in 2013. Now I'd like to share some of the circumstances surrounding the move and how the Holy Spirit supernaturally confirmed specific steps.

It was a massive faith step for CK and me. We pulled up roots and moved to another state just because an angel said the Lord wanted us to. It required leaving friends and family, as well as the comfort of an established ministry. It also took faith for our adult son Bryan to quit his job, move with us at the Spirit's leading, and help in our next phase of ministry.

The three of us joined our hearts and minds to evaluate and coordinate everything we could relating to the move. I figured we had enough finances to cover the cost of the move and six months of conservative living in Las Vegas. We fully expected supernatural provision from the Lord.

After all, this was His idea, so He had to have supernatural plans for us.

The whole process took three months. Without going into endless detail, I'll just say the enemy didn't want us to obey the call. From the get-go, we were buffeted from every side. Nothing came easily. The work involved was twice as hard as we expected, and everything cost more than it should have. The spiritual warfare was intense. To do what the Lord asked, we had to push through by faith.

By the time we were finally in our new place in Las Vegas, most of our money was used up, including our reserve for living expenses. We had fully expected to hit the ground running, as we had done several times before. After decades of ministry, we knew how to build a work for Jesus. But this was a different experience for us. We immediately began seeking the Lord for instructions on where, how, and when to launch. To our surprise, none of us had a release in the Spirit. In supernatural ministry it's critical to make sure the Holy Spirit is leading when you act. If He's not, you'll likely crash and burn, even if your motives are right.

For six months we waited on the Lord and prayed. We did a weekly YouTube video to keep in touch with some of our partners. Even when our reserves were depleted, we trusted the Lord's instruction. Supernatural faith continued to rise from within us; we believed that God had a plan and was working in all this. For six months He miraculously sustained us. Like Elijah being fed by ravens in the wilderness, we received provision from a variety of sources, as certain believers explained that the Holy Spirit told them to give to our ministry.

Then, one day while I drove home from a routine trip

to the post office, the Lord spoke loudly and clearly within my spirit, "It's go time!"

As soon as I got home, I found CK and told her that the Lord spoke to me. Before I could tell her what He spoke, she said, "It's go time! The Lord told me while you were gone."

I said, "Let's call Bryan and see if he has heard from the Lord."

I called and asked Bryan, "Are you picking up anything in the Spirit today?"

He simply said, "It's go time!"

Immediately, we rented a meeting room in a local hotel, put an ad in the newspaper, and held our first public meeting in Las Vegas. The rest is history.

Looking back on that experience, we are so thankful for the leading of the Holy Spirit and for His perfect timing. Since that first meeting, the Lord's favor has been on our ministry, and our influence has grown beyond what we imagined. It's never been about us and our plans; it has been about obeying His lead and allowing Him to flow through us, His vessels. We didn't initiate any of this. We simply followed the Holy Spirit, step by step. Today, we are reaping the rewards of standing in faith during a trying time, when all we had to go on was a word from the Lord.

A PROPHET'S PERSPECTIVE OF FAITH

In the previous chapter we discovered that God's grace is His assurance that His promises are absolute and that He will back them up. We also saw that faith is the assurance that we'll receive the manifestation of a promise. But how does faith do that?

As I said about grace, my perspective of faith comes from decades of studying God's Word and watching it play out in my spiritual experiences. Chapter 11 of Hebrews is sometimes called "The Who's Who of Faith." It testifies to us of many Old Testament saints who walked out their faith before God. The same principles that held true for their faith apply to us, as New Testament saints. Let's look at the first three verses of Hebrews 11 with that in mind.

> Now faith is the substance of things hoped for, the evidence of things not seen. For by it the elders obtained a good testimony. By faith we understand that the worlds were framed by the word of God, so that the things which are seen were not made of things which are visible.
>
> —HEBREWS 11:1–3

By way of overview, faith operates in the unseen realm and causes things to become real in the seen realm. By faith we believe that God framed the worlds in the past, touches the circumstances of our present lives, and is involved in our futures. In the passage we just read, spiritual faith is called a *substance*, meaning there's a spiritual reality to it that goes beyond mere thoughts or reasoning.

Spiritual faith and natural faith are not the same. Natural faith bases itself on natural reasoning. Through experience we can develop natural faith in people who have proved themselves trustworthy to us. We can believe in systems such as a judicial system. We can trust the living room couch not to collapse under us when we sit down.

Spiritual faith is different because its essence is spiritual. The writer to the Hebrews said, "Faith is the substance of things hoped for." The Amplified Bible, Classic Edition says, "Faith is the assurance (the confirmation, the title deed) of the things [we] hope for." The Greek word translated "substance" in many versions is *hupŏstasis*. It primarily means "assurance,"[1] which supports the role of faith in assuring the manifestation of what the Spirit reveals to us. According to Strong's Definitions, however, the word *substance*, or *hupŏstasis*, relates to "essence." It is "a setting under ([or a] support)" and is "(figuratively) concretely, essence, or abstractly, assurance (objectively or subjectively)." It's also described as "confidence, confident, person, [and] substance."[2]

Both *substance* and *assurance* are fine to use, but there is a reason I'm explaining all this.

In 2020 the world underwent an intense trauma because of the COVID-19 pandemic and the draconian overreach of government entities. The Christian church was persecuted, and many believers thought we were on the cusp of the tribulation period. Fear gripped the minds of Christians as all kinds of irrational beliefs and prophecies were spewed.

One prophecy said that Jesus would come back before the end of 2020. Another prophecy claimed that America would be attacked and that Chinese tanks would enter Washington, DC, by December of that year. Others prophesied that we were in the great tribulation. Still more prophecies for 2020 and 2021 were about the total collapse of the banking industry, the building of concentration camps to incarcerate Christians, and the devolving of the United States into a third world nation.

As a variety of voices uttered these gloom and doom prophecies, my spirit bore witness with none of them.

When I started speaking against such fear-driven declarations, I took a lot of heat. Amid my concern the Holy Spirit showed me how Jesus was protecting His church and leading it through the difficulties.

One day while I was in prayer, the Lord spoke to me about what I was hearing. He said, "Prophecies and revelations that come from the human soul, rather than the Holy Spirit, have no substance. Those prophecies are full of fear but empty of revelation and contain nothing to cause faith. Faith is the substance of prophetic revelation. Prophecy must have substance to be from Me."

It was as though a bomb went off inside me. My revelation receptors were hearing many things about faith and prophecy. But the major thing I realized was that within revelations Jesus desires to have increasingly close fellowship with us—the kind of fellowship through which everything He reveals by His Spirit bonds us to Him at the levels of our spiritual hearts. And through that process, we become more similar to Him each day. Paul put it this way: "Now the Lord is the Spirit; and where the Spirit of the Lord is, there is liberty. But we all, with unveiled face, beholding as in a mirror the glory of the Lord, are being transformed into the same image from glory to glory, just as by the Spirit of the Lord" (2 Cor. 3:17–18).

In my experience what the Holy Spirit prophetically reveals to me usually comes through the vehicle of God's Word or the voice of the Spirit, or a dream, vision, or angelic encounter. The revelation can be about the Lord, myself, others, demonic strategies, or future events. As we've seen, the encounter, in whatever form it comes, reveals a revelation room with walls, a ceiling, a floor, and a door. At the same time, the Spirit of grace fills the atmosphere of the place.

Looking more closely, I realize that the Lord is the Spirit, and Jesus is in the place! He's inviting me to join Him there; His substance is there, and He wants me to bring my substance. I can do that only by entering through the door of faith. When I do, Jesus is pleased (Heb. 11:6). He longs to fellowship with me in His mysteries. He knows that these connections are not only about things happening on the earth but also about having intimacy with Him. When we are both in the space, anything is possible and miracles occur. As "Jesus said to [the father of a convulsing boy], 'If you can believe, all things are possible to him who believes'" (Mark 9:23).

THE FAITH OF GOD

During the last week of His life, Jesus cursed a fig tree on His way to Jerusalem. The next day He and His disciples walked back by that tree and found it withered from the roots up. The disciples marveled, so Jesus told them to "have faith in God" (Mark 11:22; see also vv. 12–14, 20–21). The Greek text, however, reads, "Have the faith of God."[3] The Bible in Basic English reads, "Have God's faith."

Biblical scholar and theologian John Gill explains Jesus' phrase from Mark 11:22.

> Have faith in God...or "the faith of God," so the
> Vulgate Latin, Syriac, Persic, and Ethiopic versions;
> that is, exercise, and make use of that faith which
> has God for its author, which is the work of God,
> and of his operation, a free grace gift of his; and
> which has God for its object; and is supported by

> his power, and encouraged by his goodness, truth, and faithfulness.[4]

In other words, don't simply have faith in God, but have the God kind of faith. It's not the head faith that's born of natural reasoning; it's spiritual faith that "calls those things which do not exist as though they did" (Rom. 4:17).

Faith always precedes a manifested miracle but follows prophetic revelation. Faith assures us of the manifestation because it provides us with substance about what the Spirit is revealing. My working definition of *faith* is this: *Faith is the unwavering trust and motivating energy produced by fixing our hearts on God's Word and by seizing God's promises and power to make them realities in our lives.*

Once after speaking at an Aglow women's meeting, I began to minister through the spiritual gifts. As I looked across the audience, the Holy Spirit spiritually revealed things to me about certain people. Then I told them what the Spirit said and prayed for them in accordance with the revelations. One by one the Spirit healed, delivered, and encouraged those dear believers. At one point I came to a middle-aged woman who I felt by the Spirit had some kind of leadership anointing on her life. So I focused on her for a moment. By the Spirit I saw something wrong with her lower back, and then I saw a car. I heard the Spirit say, "Car wreck."

Going with the flow of anointing, I said to her, "The Holy Spirit just told me that you were in an automobile accident several years ago and sustained a lower-back injury. You are still experiencing pain, and the entire ordeal has tried to rob you of some of your effectiveness in leadership anointing. Is that correct?"

The woman answered immediately. She said that I was indeed a prophet and that everything I said was totally correct. She told me she was a pastor's wife and that the injury kept her from doing all that she wanted to do for the Lord. I laid hands on her and prayed the prayer of faith. God finished her healing on the spot. Through this experience her husband and I became friends.

Spiritual gifting is the container for revelation, but it is not the substance or assurance of revelation. Faith is. The Holy Spirit can lead us and show us great things all day long, but nothing will happen unless we act boldly with the God kind of faith. For this woman's miracle to happen, I had to have faith in many things—faith that the Spirit would use me, faith that He was showing me her need, faith that it was not a figment of my imagination, faith to speak forth what the Spirit showed me, and faith to pray for the woman, believing that she would be miraculously healed.

Faith Brings Us into Proper Alignment

One day I found myself facing a troubling situation. It was one of those unexpected issues that grips your gut and torments your mind. No matter what I tried, I couldn't shake it, even when I rebuked the torment and attempted to cast the thoughts out of my mind. It felt as though the battle was lost, and I was sinking into despair.

That's when I heard the voice of the Lord deep inside my gut. He asked, "Do you remember what My Word says concerning an unclean spirit that goes out of a man and seeks rest in dry places?" (Matt. 12:43).

"Yes, Lord," I responded. "It's in Matthew 12."

"There is a principle I wish for you to learn." The Lord

continued, "When the unclean spirit discovers that his former home is empty and available, he moves right back in and takes seven other unclean spirits with him (vv. 44–45). That makes things worse. Casting out a spirit and leaving the place empty is the mistake. You must fill the void with the Holy Spirit and the things of God so there is no place to which the unclean spirit can return."

"Yes, Lord."

He continued, "The most effective way to do this is through displacement. Use My Word, along with praise and worship, to push the spirit out. Do that in faith. The place will then be filled with godly things, and the spirit won't be able to torment you any longer."

"Thank You, Lord, for this revelation," I said.

Immediately I started quoting aloud and at the top of my lungs every verse from the Word that I knew. In between verses I prayed in tongues, preached to myself, and worshipped the Lord for His goodness and faithfulness. I also decreed what my faith had to say about the situation. After forty-five minutes to an hour of putting nonstop pressure on the mental torment I was experiencing, it broke. The lying spirits were displaced, peace came, and my fearful emotions turned into confidence and victory. My mind was now full of faith in God.

In the natural realm we are both rational and emotional beings. There is nothing wrong with this, because God formed us that way. However, when you are out of proper alignment, problems can arise in your spiritual life. To be rational is to be capable of reasoning or logic. This is the objective side of your physical being. To be emotional means to be capable of feeling and moods. This is the subjective side of your physical being.

Although maintaining the proper balance between being rational and being emotional is an age-old quest, we can openly observe how the issue affects society today. For sixty or more years the pendulum in America has swung from a more objective posture (which guided our nation through its formative years) to a more subjective one. As a result, a person's intelligence quotient is perceived to be less important than one's emotional quotient. This is why we have watched almost everything be reevaluated and redefined to fit our feelings rather than reason. Our nation's constitution, laws, government, and basic systems, which were formed by logic, are being threatened, with large segments of society claiming that those national things don't feel fair. These segments of society no longer have faith in such things, because emotions can't produce faith.

Now, let's transfer those principles to the Christian life. God's kind of faith bases itself on spiritual reason. God's Word—His *logos*, or His *rhema*—is truth, regardless of how we feel. So here is an interesting dynamic: Faith emerges when we deeply trust God's Word in our spirits, allowing His Word to shape our rational thoughts and steer our emotions. This harmony turns our emotions into forces that support our faith rather than hinder it. Because faith brings us into alignment, our emotions can then infuse us with the energies we need to walk out our faith.

Emotions play an important part in interpreting prophetic experiences. During the communication process the Holy Spirit connects with our feelings. He can touch our emotions or even superimpose His feelings over ours. Understanding a prophetic experience requires you to pay attention to what your feelings are telling you as the revelation is occurring. However, once the revelation is received, faith requires your feelings to come in line with the Spirit's instructions.

The Form of the Lord

My final point concerning the ways of the Spirit is about the form of the Lord. Most Spirit-filled believers, especially those who may read this book, desperately want to see Jesus and hear His voice. While we readily acknowledge that the Holy Spirit is involved in our lives, our hearts still long for our Savior to speak to us. I've learned, however, that it isn't a matter of *whether* He speaks to us; it is a matter of recognizing *how* He speaks to us.

Learning the form of the Lord is a giant step forward in walking in the spiritual realm. The Lord got angry when Aaron and Miriam wickedly spoke against Moses and justified themselves by saying that God spoke to them too. Here's part of what the Lord said to them: "If there is a prophet among you, I, the LORD, make Myself known to him in a vision; I speak to him in a dream. Not so with My servant Moses; he is faithful in all My house. I speak with him face to face, even plainly, and not in dark sayings; and he sees *the form of the* LORD" (Num. 12:6–8).

Here, the Lord acknowledged that He talked to other prophets. Remember that this was an Old Covenant text. Therefore, the indwelling presence of the Holy Spirit was not yet available to all believers, as it would be under the New Covenant. The point, however, is that the Lord also revealed that He talked differently to Moses, who saw "the form of the LORD." The Lord spoke to Moses through a burning bush only *after* Moses perceived something supernatural and turned to investigate it. "When the LORD saw that he turned aside to look, God called to him from the midst of the bush" (Exod. 3:4).

Spiritually speaking, how many burning bushes have we passed by while saying, "The Lord doesn't speak to me"? If we would perceive the form of the Lord, He would speak. He spoke to Balaam through a donkey and to Elijah through a still, small voice. The Lord speaks to everyone differently. Learning how He speaks to you is the key to unlocking the gifts of the Spirit and ministering to others. But more importantly, it's the key to hearing His voice in sweet communion and fellowship and in His shepherding.

The form of the Lord has two aspects. We see both aspects in Paul's words to the Philippians: "Let this mind be in you which was also in Christ Jesus, who, being in the *form* of God, did not consider it robbery to be equal with God, but made Himself of no reputation, taking the *form* of a bond-servant, and coming in the likeness of men" (Phil. 2:5–7).

The word *form* there is the Greek *morphē*.[5] The primary aspect of form is essence, or nature (not shape). Jesus possessed the essence of God. The secondary aspect of form is the shape that the essence takes. Jesus took the form of a man. As a servant His essence spoke to humanity. He spoke to Mary Magdalene and appeared in the form of a gardener (John 20:11–17); He spoke to the two travelers on the road to Emmaus, appearing to them in the form of a teacher (Luke 24:13–35).

Those are biblical examples, but what about the subtler ways He speaks to us, such as through a song or a gentle breeze? He can speak through the voice of a spouse or through Bible verses that suddenly come alive to us. Regardless of the form's shape, we are looking for the essence of His voice.

As prophets CK and I take nothing for granted. We've learned to perceive the form of the Lord anywhere and anytime. If you are endeavoring to figure out how to discern the Lord's voice from the Holy Spirit's voice, I simply say that it really doesn't matter, because they are of the same essence. The point is to learn how you hear God's voice. That is the way of the Spirit for you.

One hot summer day while I was writing this book, the temperature in Las Vegas was 110 degrees. But around noontime, dark clouds suddenly blew in, thunder crashed, and the sky opened up. I used this refreshing downpour to take a short break and watch the rain through my window. The storm lasted for about an hour. Then, just as fast as it came, it went. The rain stopped, the clouds parted, and the sun beamed through. While peering out the window, I heard the voice that's become so familiar to me; it was the Lord's voice unexpectedly speaking within my heart. He said, "I am sending My rain upon the earth. Though you've been enduring the storm for a while, its dark clouds and fierce winds will soon give way to refreshing rain. This rain will cleanse the filth and decay, bringing renewal. When the storm clouds disperse, a new day and new life will emerge. Stay vigilant and pray for the outpouring of My Spirit. When it comes suddenly, seize it quickly. Treasure it as a gift of healing from heaven. Countless souls will be saved and welcomed into My kingdom, and there will be great rejoicing among the angels and saints."

LION'S ARMY, ARISE!

This is the time of the Lion's army. Evil and darkness have risen in ways that most could not have imagined even a decade ago. The enemy's strategies have been clever and somewhat effective. Jesus was not caught off guard, however, and His Spirit was not asleep. The all-knowing and all-powerful Godhead is raising a standard against the darkness. Part of the standard is the army of Spirit-filled, prophetic believers that the Spirit introduced to me as the Lion's army.

The Lion's army is a prophetic army of warriors who run with the glory of God upon them. They rise into the heavenlies and use third-heaven authority in their warfare. They use spiritual energies, with fire, light, and wind as weapons in their mouths. They battle in the unseen realm for the souls of men and women and for the destinies of nations. This army has learned the mysteries of Jesus' kingdom and the ways of the Spirit.

And when the Lion of Judah roars with boldness and authority, His army declares to every demon, "You have lost. We have won!"

NOTES

Chapter 1: The Lion's Army

1. "Acts 10:10: Barnes' Notes on the Bible," Bible Hub, accessed September 25, 2024, https://biblehub.com/commentaries/acts/10-10.htm.

Chapter 2: The Ways of the Spirit

1. Mike Thompson, *Third-Heaven Authority: Discover How to Pray from Heaven's Perspective* (Charisma House, 2023), 158–159.
2. Thompson, *Third-Heaven Authority*, 159–160.
3. Blue Letter Bible, s.v. "*derek*," accessed September 18, 2024, https://www.blueletterbible.org/lexicon/h1870/kjv/wlc/0-1/; Blue Letter Bible, s.v. "*hodos*," accessed September 18, 2024, https://www.blueletterbible.org/lexicon/g3598/kjv/tr/0-1/.

Chapter 3: More Lion's Army Visions

1. Thompson, *Third-Heaven Authority*, 175, 178, 190.

Chapter 5: The Believer's Makeup

1. Gary H. Everett, *Study Notes on the Holy Scriptures: The Epistle of 1 Thessalonians* (n.p., 2024), 160.
2. Blue Letter Bible, s.v. "*pneuma*," accessed September 23, 2024, https://www.blueletterbible.org/lexicon/g4151/kjv/tr/0-1/.
3. Bible Study Tools, s.v. "Psuche," accessed October 7, 2024, https://www.biblestudytools.com/lexicons/greek/kjv/psuche.html#:~:text=Psuche%20Definition&text=the%20seat%20of%20the%20feelings,our%20heart%2C%20soul%20etc.
4. Blue Letter Bible, s.v. "*psychē*," accessed September 23, 2024, https://www.blueletterbible.org/lexicon/g5590/kjv/tr/0-1/; Bible Study Tools, s.v. "Psuche."
5. Bible Study Tools, s.v. "Psuche"; Blue Letter Bible, s.v. "*psychē*."
6. Blue Letter Bible, s.v. "*sōma*," accessed September 23, 2024, https://www.blueletterbible.org/lexicon/g4983/kjv/tr/0-1/.
7. Blue Letter Bible, s.v. "*sōma*."

8. Kapil Sachdeva, "11 Fun Facts About Your Brain: 3 Pounds of Remarkable Matter," Northwestern Medicine, accessed October 8, 2024, https://www.nm.org/healthbeat/healthy-tips/11-fun-facts-about-your-brain.
9. Julie Bartucca, "The Most Complicated Object in the Universe," UConn Today, March 16, 2018, https://today.uconn.edu/2018/03/complicated-object-universe/.
10. Wikipedia, s.v. "Perception," accessed September 24, 2024, https://en.wikipedia.org/wiki/Perception.

Chapter 7: Spiritual Gifts, Part 1

1. Blue Letter Bible, s.v. "*pneumatikos*," accessed September 25, 2024, https://www.blueletterbible.org/lexicon/g4152/kjv/tr/0-1/.
2. Blue Letter Bible, s.v. "*pneumatikos*."
3. Albert Barnes, "1 Corinthians 12: Barnes' Notes on the Whole Bible," StudyLight.org, accessed September 25, 2024, https://www.studylight.org/commentaries/eng/bnb/1-corinthians-12.html.
4. Marvin Vincent, "1 Corinthians 12: Vincent's Word Studies," StudyLight.org, accessed September 25, 2024, https://www.studylight.org/commentaries/eng/vnt/1-corinthians-12.html.

Chapter 8: Spiritual Gifts, Part 2

1. WebMD Editorial Contributors, "What Is Hematidrosis?," WebMD, accessed September 26, 2024, https://www.webmd.com/a-to-z-guides/hematidrosis-hematohidrosis.

Chapter 9: A New Christian Era

1. Blue Letter Bible, s.v. "*syschēmatizō*," accessed September 30, 2024, https://www.blueletterbible.org/lexicon/g4964/kjv/tr/0-1/; Blue Letter Bible, s.v. "*schēma*," accessed September 27, 2024, https://www.blueletterbible.org/lexicon/g4976/kjv/mgnt/0-1/#lexResults; Blue Letter Bible, "Dictionaries: Fashion, C-2 Verb—Strong's Number: G4964," accessed September 30, 2024, https://www.blueletterbible.org/search/Dictionary/viewTopic.cfm?topic=VT0001002; *Dictionary of Biblical Languages with Semantic Domains: Greek (New Testament)*, s.v. "syschēmatizō."

2. Curt Hinkle, "Metamorfoo," *Practical Theology Today*, accessed September 30, 2024, https://practicaltheologytoday.com/2019/03/26/metamorfoo/.

3. Blue Letter Bible, s.v. "*rāḥap̄*," accessed September 30, 2024, https://www.blueletterbible.org/lexicon/h7363/niv/wlc/0-1/.

4. FIRM Staff, "Ruach and the Hebrew Word for the Holy Spirit," Fellowship of Israel Related Ministries, accessed September 30, 2024, https://firmisrael.org/learn/ruach-the-hebrew-word-for-holy-spirit/.

5. Bible Study Tools, s.v. "Pneuma," accessed November 19, 2024, https://www.biblestudytools.com/lexicons/greek/kjv/pneuma.html.

6. *Merriam-Webster*, s.v. "brood," accessed September 30, 2024, https://www.merriam-webster.com/dictionary/brood.

7. Blue Letter Bible, s.v. "*episkiazō*," accessed September 30, 2024, https://www.blueletterbible.org/lexicon/g1982/kjv/tr/0-1/.

CHAPTER 10: SPIRIT-FILLED BELIEVERS
MAKE THE BEST WARRIORS

1. Blue Letter Bible, s.v. "*rēma*," accessed October 7, 2024, https://www.blueletterbible.org/lexicon/g4487/kjv/tr/0-1/.

CHAPTER 11: GRACE IS THE ASSURANCE
OF A PROPHETIC LIFE

1. Charles Haddon Spurgeon, "Morning, May 16," Christian Classics Ethereal Library, accessed October 3, 2024, https://www.ccel.org/ccel/spurgeon/morneve.d0516am.html.

2. Blue Letter Bible, s.v. "*logos*," accessed October 3, 2024, https://www.blueletterbible.org/lexicon/g3056/kjv/tr/0-1/.

3. Blue Letter Bible, s.v. "*rēma*."

CHAPTER 12: FAITH IS THE SUBSTANCE OF A PROPHETIC LIFE

1. Blue Letter Bible, s.v. "*hypostasis*," accessed October 4, 2024, https://www.blueletterbible.org/lexicon/g5287/kjv/tr/0-1/.

2. Blue Letter Bible, s.v. "*hypostasis*."

3. "Mark 11:22—Pulpit Commentary," Bible Hub, accessed October 4, 2024, https://biblehub.com/mark/11-22.htm. Some Bibles, such as the Cambridge Bible, note the Hebrew text in the margin.

4. "John Gill's Exposition of the Bible: Mark 11:22," Bible Study Tools, accessed October 4, 2024, https://www.biblestudytools.com/commentaries/gills-exposition-of-the-bible/mark-11-22.html.
5. Blue Letter Bible, s.v. *"morphē,"* accessed October 4, 2024, https://www.blueletterbible.org/lexicon/g3444/kjv/tr/0-1/.

I pray this book encourages you to learn the ways of the Spirit so you may wage a good warfare.

—MIKE THOMPSON

mikethompsonministries.org

Rejoice always, pray without ceasing, in everything give thanks; for this is the will of God in Christ Jesus for you. Do not quench the Spirit. Do not despise prophecies. Test all things; hold fast what is good. Abstain from every form of evil. Now may the God of peace Himself sanctify you completely; and may your whole spirit, soul, and body be preserved blameless at the coming of our Lord Jesus Christ.

—1 Thessalonians 5:16–23

My **FREE GIFT** to You

Dear Readers,

As a token of my appreciation and to share God's truth, I'm offering you a FREE eBook version of *Third Heaven Authority*!

— TO GAIN ACCESS TO YOUR GIFT —

MYCHARISMASHOP.COM/PAGES/THOMPSON-GIFT-2025

BLESSINGS TO YOU,

Mike Thompson